The Paper Lantern

Will Burns is a poet and writer based in Buckinghamshire. He began publishing his poetry in 2014 when he was named a Faber & Faber New Poet, and since then he has also published poetry pamphlets with Clutag Press, Rough Trade Books and his first full collection, *Country Music*, with Offord Road Books in 2020.

Will is a long-time contributor to the online nature-writing journal *Caught by the River*, and his work has been discussed in the *Guardian*, the *Times Literary Supplement*, *Poetry Review* and the *Independent*.

The Paper Lantern

Will Burns

WEIDENFELD & NICOLSON

First published in Great Britain in 2021
by Weidenfeld & Nicolson
an imprint of The Orion Publishing Group Ltd
Carmelite House, 50 Victoria Embankment
London EC4Y 0DZ

An Hachette UK Company

1 3 5 7 9 10 8 6 4 2

A CIP catalogue record for this book is
available from the British Library.

ISBN (Hardback) 978 1 4746 2202 8
ISBN (eBook) 978 1 4746 2204 2
ISBN (Trade Paperback) 978 1474 62465 7
ISBN (Audio) 978 1 7462 2059

Printed and bound in Great Britain by Clays Ltd, Elcograf, S.p.A

www.orionbooks.co.uk
www.weidenfeldandnicolson.co.uk

In memory of

Jonathan Coles
30.12.1980 – 11.6.1999

*and dedicated to his
friends and family*

Acknowledgements

I am hugely grateful to Carl Gosling, Robin Turner
and all involved with The Social Gathering for
initial and ongoing encouragement, to Declan Ryan
for his generosity, time and unerring eye and to
Nina Hervé for all that plus her infinite patience,
inspiration and love.

I owe Lee Brackstone enormous thanks for helping
shape the first unwieldy chunks of this writing
into the book it has become.

Thanks also to Ellie Freedman, and everyone
at Weidenfeld & Nicolson, Martha Sprackland,
Becky Thomas, my parents and the regulars at
'The Paper Lantern'.

In July I am stiff and dead and irreconcilable,

a mad-dog wind tore my miserable earth apart,

I am sworn to this time of every reeking condition!

—Thomas Bernhard, 'In July'

Part One

Paradox, Bedrock

The only reasonable way to begin, I suppose, is with
a rough physical description. The place with which
we are concerned was a small market town which,
for some reason that nobody could ever adequately
explain to me, insisted upon being called a village.
You might well ask how a place could insist on such
a thing – or, indeed, give voice to speak its insistence.
Already, then, we have hit upon a point of interest
– did the place have some innate sense of self?
Did it make demands of those who lived within its
boundaries, did it impose its will on the people of the
place, did it somehow impress upon their collective
imagination its essential village-ness? Perhaps we
shall see. For now, it's enough to know that the
inhabitants of this place called it a village and so,
in the interests of conciliation, will I. But let's return
to the physical facts. The topographical design. The
surface of things. The high street ran from east to west

on a small incline up into the hills that surrounded the village. It was a high street of no real consequence, the same as any number of similar streets in any number of small towns and villages across the country. The large coaching inn halfway down had become, by then, a tired yet expensive hotel. There were three charity shops, a florist, a small Italian restaurant, a couple of curry houses (either excellent or terrible, depending on who you asked), four or five hairdressers, one a large salon-type affair that offered all the usual supplementary ministrations – the removal of body hair, the augmentation of fingernails and toenails, facial treatments. If you walked across the top of Coombe Hill, which rose at the eastern edge of the village and had one of those pleasingly tautological place names that attach themselves to natural features of the landscape, and down to the bottom of the next valley you would find yourself at Chequers, which had long been the country residence of whoever was the current prime minister. Please don't think I mention this fact as anything like a boast. You will, perhaps, become aware that this is not the sort of thing to which I attached any real importance, much less would crow about. Plenty in the village would do, though. For my part, I mention it merely to add to our understanding of the consciousness the place had of itself. Of its own status and specificity in the scheme of all other possible places. Because here, at least the proximity of this notable residence seemed to suggest, was a kind of eminence, a grandeur, though the village, it was true, carried that status lightly, wore it in a modest, suburban way. It was close enough to London for the high rollers of the city to escape to, but with all the trappings of what had become known as the country. Which meant, more or less, monoculture arable farming, a designation of some scientific interest in the topography, lots of walkers and cyclists and their attendant synthetic fibres, dogs of all shapes and sizes, bad pubs, good pubs, mediocre pubs and, importantly in this particular case, a school system which had for a number of decades attracted a dull and rapacious middle class who appeared to me to propagate themselves on a particular kind of mutual congratulation and self-satisfaction. And yet on the other hand there was also a sense of them having settled in some way for something slightly below their own expectations. They spoke at times as if they were apologising for having found themselves living there in that unspectacular, rather tame place. They talked of their past lives and their adventurous youths. Their lost hedonism. Now, though, all they did, having of course reproduced, was to eat and drink and travel then talk, seemingly endlessly, about where they had eaten and what they had drunk and where they had travelled. Fair enough, I might have been able to bring myself to say to the people when I saw them. What more should they have done with their time, after all.

For my part, life tended to organise itself more often than not around the drinking aspect of things –

specifically in a pub called The Paper Lantern which, helpfully, was run by my parents. Or more accurately, I should say, it *had* been run by them until those first hallucinatory and long, lonely weeks when, along with everything else in the country, the pub had been made to close its doors while the virus that had taken hold around the world was attempting to be dealt with. In the time after the country shut up shop, I am bound to admit here, I indulged myself somewhat. I began to take walks that were longer than strictly allowed in those early days of what had become known as 'the lockdown', and I found myself living a kind of dream-life. Of course, it says something about the place in which I lived that in the first month or so, when the big cities were in the midst of privations and anxieties and traumas barely imaginable only a short time previously, there had been almost no news locally of any deaths, no hard facing up to the real, terrible impact of the disease. We heard early on that a man who had until the year before owned one of the curry houses had died. Since selling up, word was that he had moved away, back to where his family lived in a large town in the next county. Other than that, our provincial rumour had been benign. And news always seemed to spread here as anecdote, rather than through the rigour of anything as sensible or intelligent as research, much like what passed, at times, for objective reality. We were, for instance, in the heart of Brexit-country, the safest Tory seat in the house and over the previous couple of years, had you engaged in conversation with any one of the know-alls in any one of the village's pubs you would have got the secondhand opinions or dimly recollected experiences of Europe, or the EU, foreigners, which they touted as hard empirical evidence of how things really stood. I had no doubt there were those among the villagers who were secretly jubilant to find themselves in the situation they did when the virus forced the government's hand and a global disaster unfolded. A generation of people who had always struggled to define themselves against the terms of their parents' totemic conflicts finally had their own war. On the radio I heard about the disease's capacity for exposing the faultlines of inequality, and in the village I bore witness to it in the disease's invisibility, its uncanny quality of being both everywhere and nowhere. Out here, away from the cities, there was a sense that the whole thing was a kind of long bank holiday.

I was implicated myself, of course, in this bloated malaise – I had to admit I was pleased at the prospect of weeks without having to drag myself to a dreary part-time job, days of walking, reading and perhaps even being able to write. There was a vague and listless guilt at the thought, too, of finding satisfaction in such time. Then again, I found myself simply resenting the ominous return of a life in which my worth was totted up to £8.21 an hour and came with all that we previously believed so hard in, and about which I had, shall we say, some doubts concerning the nature of work and money and status. For a few weeks, these things became a kind of locus for national thought, for national discussion. What would be there when we eventually got back to what we'd once called so affectionately, so needily, 'work'?

Before the virus, I worked part-time in the Lantern and tried to write my wretched little poems and was well used to the odd looks people could not stop themselves giving a thirty-nine-year-old man working in his parents' pub. Seeing a fully grown adult seemingly happy to live on that meagre wage was not necessarily the cause of consternation, it was more that the true currency around there, the currency which I was perceived to have so little respect for, was status. This manifested itself in a variety of ways. There were the obvious – the cars, the houses, the jobs, the holidays. But there were many other playing fields, none more vicious and competitive than the selective education system which in turn made the area so desirable. In the pub you could hear parents talking about private tuition, extra classes, past exam papers and maths coaches, desperate as they were for their children to pass the 11-plus and get to the local grammar school. Their faces had the strained, serious bearing that all the thirty-to-forty-somethings in the village showed when they discussed the important issues of the day over a pint or a gin and tonic. Their latest life-changing nutritional discovery, their utterly understandable, utterly reasonable, utterly pragmatic politics, the ecological and economic considerations of their multiple holiday destinations, their new cars, their recent cycling trips, their marathon training.

The lockdown coincided with a fine, sunny spring. We'd had a miserable and sodden winter and the relief was palpable when a bit of warm weather arrived. (Palpable how? Was the place giving voice again?) With the pub closed I no longer saw my fellow residents every day, and so no longer exchanged gossip and pleasantries and platitudes or through that contact heard what might be called the voice of the place. Instead we saw each other every now and then in the queue that formed each morning outside the pharmacy and the little supermarket on the high street, or down at the allotments, or out walking in the hills. A brief hello and an ask after my parents and the pub. Thank God for the sunshine. Strange times. See you when I see you. I had also signed up to be available as community help should it be needed in my 'three-street zone', and so was sent a regular warden's email with details of various local support groups and other information concerning the local effort – the small successes, the potential stress-points and a little motivational bluster. Each email began with a statement about the weather. I'm sure if I stretched for it there would be a clever point to be made about our ever-changing relationship to the elemental things of the world, how our new circumstances might have provided an opportunity to achieve some new and

more fundamental, more sympathetic knowledge
of the earth beyond our own human realm. But I
suspected people mentioned the weather simply out
of necessity, out of a hope of avoiding more talk of the
virus and lockdowns and isolation. Perhaps simply out
of habit. Out of a lack of imagination. I hoped in those
first weeks that a change of some kind might come to
pass, that we would, through our new experience and
conception of time and even of ourselves, come to know
better the weather systems, the hills, the fields and
streams and life of the place, of all our places. I had
certainly become aware of people noticing the songs of
birds, acquiring the names of local plants, picking wild
garlic in the woods and developing a deeper interest
in their gardens. The allotments in the village looked
so well tended and presentable they could have come
out of a book.

I couldn't say for sure what it was that made me think
at that time about the poet-philosopher Tim Lilburn.
He had once been recommended to me by my oldest
friend Stephen the first Christmas he came back to
the village from university. Perhaps something about
the uncanny dislocation of ourselves from one another,
the proposition of a life in the immediate term that
would, for how long we could not know, have some
sort of monastic property – solitude, thought, silence,
all made me think of his work. He wrote invoking
paradise, the original garden, and a desire, an 'eros'
we all feel for what had been lost in the Fall. A desire

that manifests as a kind of homesickness. There was some of this, I thought, in how people talked about the world they had known just a few weeks ago, and the longing they felt for it. And yet there was something of it too in the rediscovery, the little advancements, of a novel relationship with the natural world that was, and always had been, so very close. People were forced to reckon with what they missed, and what they might never have realised they missed. So I found myself, despite luxuriating in a sudden lack of waged labour, and in a glut of what was once called leisure time, homesick for certain elements of the pub. The week before he finally called for a closure of shops, bars and restaurants, the Prime Minister, with a trademark mixture of false bonhomie and overconfidence, invoked 'the inalienable right of free-born people of the United Kingdom to go to the pub'. The phrase was a gory mess and yet the primacy of his image in that moment was telling. Despite its ubiquity, despite its symbolic use by the tawdry politicians of the day and their cap-tugging cronies in the press, the pub remained the focal point for what had become a sudden awareness of some lack. Our own pub was full of sad, amusing, strange and sometimes disquieting types. I thought of them often, in those early days in my own company, and suddenly appreciated all of their profoundly discreet selves. The ways in which each of them ultimately resisted the categorical even while retaining certain communal similarities. Lilburn wrote of something like this – a differentiation between individual living things that was felt most hard when he experienced an animal in the wild. For our part, there was the middle-aged hippie who loved the hills and hated smartphones, with a box of his homemade pakoras for the anti-HS2 protest camp that had grown up on the outskirts of the village late last year. Here was the seven-foot biker, white beard down to his belly button, here the improbably likeable misanthropic prison guard, here the rather lost young man who worked full-time behind the bar, his head anachronistically full of banal bar-room opinion and pointless pub-quiz knowledge, here the quiche-and-pie lady, her name on a bottle of Chardonnay in the bottom of the fridge, and who every now and again asked, conspiratorially, towards the end of the night, for a large brandy to slip into her wine glass. And here was the woman whose daughter had played Tina Turner in a recent London musical and who had taken a few other regulars to see the show, and whose conversation every now and then betrayed her frustrations at the more sinister aspects of Home Counties homogeneity. In simple terms, I supposed, there was a yearning for the return of some physical and emotional communal life, but beyond that, when I thought of the pub, I thought multitudinously. Then again, there were times when I thought of the regulars in the bar and they dissolved into a kind of sameness. There were nights for example when the whole saloon bar was filled with people called Pete. On one particular occasion, I recall being the only person in there not called Pete. There had always been jokes about the proliferation of that one name, what it meant about the place, what it said for the narrowness of imagination, culture, language. When a new chef from the tapas place down the road came in one evening and was standing at the bar waiting for his drink, one of the regulars asked him what his name was. The chef found it hard at first to understand why he was being asked, why they might have wanted to know about his name, what interest it could have held, let alone what humour. The whole thing seemed to have deflated slightly, the young man's confusion unsettling the joke. The Petes all fell a little quiet until the chef, shrugging, decided to give his name. Pedro, he said. My name is Pedro.

Another long morning. I opened the door onto South Street and took the white chalk path into the hills by the old wellhead again and walked and waited.

*   *   *   *

What could have been worse, I thought to myself in those first days, as the bleak reality dawned hard on all of us, the news a daily update of various catastrophes, than spending the next few months alone in a place defined by its historic communality? A fatuous idea – there is *always* a case worse off than your own, no matter how desperate one feels things might have become. And I say alone, which was also a bit of a stretch, as in fact I lived, then, in the temporarily closed and brooding old pub, with my mother and father. I was compelled to keep what had been termed a 'social' distance even indoors, and not so much because of the chance of infection, but because of the fast-fraying tempers and deteriorating psychological states of the three of us. In the initial few days of being shut up, my parents sat outside in the beer garden, my mother enjoying the sun, my father a little lost without his regulars, without his inventory of tasks – in short, without his work. They started with the cask ale which would have soon gone off if it hadn't been drunk, then moved on to gin and tonics in the afternoon, rum and gingers in the evening, and eventually, by nightfall, the bourbon. I grew a little anxious. Then again, I am bound to say that I partook myself, and that first week was a sunlit drinking spree of slippery time and the suspension of old certainties which had, almost imperceptibly, become hardships, however small. The days ended with no dread of the next, the hours passed with no impending pressure. There was, simply put, nothing to do. The roads fell silent, the small market square in the village emptied, the dismal weather of the dregs of the previous winter having broken, quite suddenly, it seemed, into the vivid skies of a soft, verdant spring. But the mix of novelty and shock and respite wore off, and we all, after a week or two, fell into line. A first drink not taken until five, that sort of thing. I could tell after those initial couple of weeks that there was something about being stuck here in the Lantern, perhaps something in the very fabric of the building itself, that was getting to the old man. The rooms, after all, carried some quintessence of their former conviviality. Their form was essentially one of congregation, of companionship. The tables and chairs, however, sat empty. It was oppressing all three of us, this absence, but my father was distracted, morbid, convinced he was spent.

Quite unlike me, my father was powered by the will to work. He had no hobbies to speak of, no interests, no pastimes. The closure of the pub was an erosion of his identity, an undermining of those things he had always, without considering them to be mutable or up for debate, believed in to the extent that he had long since come to rely upon them – utterances that had come to be his ritual invocations, truths that had come to be his tenets. Work ethic, hard work. Times of crisis were to be met squarely and simply with work and more work. They were to be fought, to acquiesce to a current vogue for militaristic invocations, and defeated with that final, triumphant, catch-all, capitalistic strategy, a strategy that had become so pervasive as to be mistaken for an aspect of culture: work. All this and his eldest child could barely get a grasp on the word. I found it too easily said, too often called upon, too uncritically deployed. I mistrusted how many and how different the meanings of the word were when I came up against them. Put simply, I had always been indolent, and it was true that I could happily lie

around all day without so much as reading a word or
raising a hand in effort. Part of me, in those days just
before it occurred, secretly desired the closure of the
pub, and with it an end to my own allocation of jobs,
to the interminable clock-watching, waiting as I
always was to get off work and round to the right
side of the bar. I found myself between two positions
– dreading the return of the endless tasks, the glass
washer, the pint-pouring, the cleaning, the stupefied
drunks and the long, slow, dead afternoons, but
still desiring the high rapture of the Lantern's old
communion at its best, the babbling background noise,
the late afternoon light caught in a half-empty glass,
the rush of laughter layered upon laughter, one wave
of it crashing upon another as the drink filled your
chest and your cheeks and the fire glowed beside
you, or sitting outside in the distended daylight of
summer's peak, still warm at closing time, the tables
rearranged as if the whole garden full of people were
one throng gathered under the huge willow tree that
acted as shelter and sentinel and that now stood
listless in the centre of the beer garden, a stack of
chairs leaning against its trunk.

Some days I watched, if that is the correct word for
observing life via the internet, the kind of people
who would – if I were of a different type, or perhaps
lived somewhere more cultivated, more urbane – be
called my peers talking about their 'work' during
the lockdown. Writers and poets who described their

experience in phrases such as *failing to keep up with work*, or *struggling with my work*. Arguably it was a failure of my own imagination, and not the first, that I was unable to conceive of a thing as *work* unless somebody else had *told* me to do it. A poet failing to 'keep up' needs simply to stop writing the poem. Nobody asked for it and it will save no one. This attitude may explain the spectacular failure of my own poems. For a little while, a few years ago, I thought that might all have worked out differently, but like every fraud, I had indulged my ego to the detriment of what turned out to be a meagre talent. And perhaps in fact there was something I had always admired in failure. The idea of success became suffocating around here from a young age, and even at school I found myself asking what it truly meant, what it looked like. I found the head boys and prefects laughable. Their puffed-up sincerity, their crawling, their desperate need for approval and their pathetic aping of authority. And outside the realm of the school, who was to arbitrate on the measure of success? All my life I had started projects and given them up. I wrote a little and quickly grew bored of my subjects. I began on some line of enquiry or other, then abandoned them all. I distrusted the motives of others, which of course in truth meant that I distrusted my own. I have had to dress my failures up in regret, for the sake of appearances, but the fact was that I never truly cared enough. About anything, perhaps. So it was that I found myself living in the spare room above my parents' pub, working

there part-time, and following the writing careers of
others on the internet with a mix of jealousy and horror
as if it were all a soap opera – the characters scarcely
believable and the interactions coming off as false,
unlived – in short, as something written.

* * * *

I took myself off into the country most mornings.
I continued to exceed the allotted exercise time
permitted, walking for hours, and later, when I
got home and listened to the news on the radio,
I wondered how I should feel about everything. Guilt?
Shame? Did I really understand these walks to be an
outrageous indulgence, the latest shape my lifelong
selfishness had taken, one that was now connected to
the deaths and suffering of others? I read about how
I was supposed to feel about things in the opinion
columns and I heard it on the radio, saw it on the
internet. But out here it was hard to tally opinion,
with its capital 'O' and its bylines and headshots, with
the divergent facts of the matter across the country.
This place simply did not feel like a place of death and
disease. It felt as comfortable as affluence always does.
And so I walked on, both implicated and exultant,
up into the hills and out of the village, up onto the
Chilterns escarpment. I took to the white chalk trail
marked on the OS map as the Ridgeway, an ancient
way that ran across the south of the country and
headed out of the village and into the surrounding hills.

The path was a commercial scar in the land, used for generations to cart goods and livestock from the farms in the east to the markets in the west. An ancient pull, then, that dragged my feet into the hills – an urge to escape the physical confines of a building denuded of its folk-purpose and the psychological enclosure of my life there, nearing forty and living with my parents – the reality of which had suddenly become brutally clear.

Early mornings on top of the hill, the birdsong rich and varied in the beech woods, the bluebells shimmering, the wild garlic pungent in the cool air, proliferating in patches here and there under the trees. I was out there long before the dog walkers, the family cycle rides, before the expensively shod and utterly comically serious runners. Half a dozen red kites glided slowly past me where the scarp dropped sharply into the valley below. Their forms in the moving air were hypnotic, something between chaos and supreme control. Economy of movement, absolute discretion in each flurry of breeze in their flight feathers. It was beyond worship, what I felt watching those birds, worship which required symbols, abstractions, and their attendant ideas. This was the keen desire for the world, felt anew. Quietude lent everything some unfamiliar aspect in which we had all begun to revel. The roads belonged to the foxes and muntjac now, and the skies to the birds. Below us, me and the kites, lay a large field with the straight white line of the Ridgeway cut across it, pulling the eye further out to the west, into the range of hills, out of the county and across to the next. The previous year the field had been full of rapeseed, but now I saw mostly groundsel and chickweed in the hard, baked earth. The farmer was, perhaps, behind with his planting, the whole field given up as a bad job for the spring, or maybe the field was simply being left fallow. The vivid yellow of the previous year's crop felt like another loss for the season, and yet at the same time another victory for the true earth, the weeds and wildflowers encroaching on the land that had in truth always belonged to them. The farmer who tended the field had cut a huge *NHS* logo into the growth with a tractor. I played five-a-side football with him on occasional Monday nights, and looking at the field I remembered the team's conversation on WhatsApp the night of the general election the previous year, and what had been said about things like socialism and public spending and magic money trees.

* * * *

One lunchtime a week or so into the lockdown I sat in the empty saloon bar with a bottle of beer on the table in front of me. However many days ago – who could say how many now that time had lost so much of its previous measure, its sense, a falsehood it turned out, as something concrete, definitive and divisible.. I recalled how that whole final evening had been coloured by the government's announcement that as of midnight that very night, pubs, restaurants, offices, shops, cafés – all, in fact, except the most essential places of work would have to close. Everybody in the pub had gone through to the larger bar to watch the press conference live on the big TV. A sense of anticipation and a perverse kind of excitement had been felt for a few days, during which we had habitually taken in these government updates, waiting for what we weren't quite sure – for the commencement of something, anything, for that exhilarating, terrifying moment of confirmation that you are witnessing history. There had been, I suppose inevitably, a peculiar quality to the rest of the night, once the something we had all been waiting for had finally arrived. The sense of an ending, some finality that people could not yet articulate, that they had not quite fully prepared themselves for and did not yet even understand. Did they, I wondered now, at that precise moment, with their prospects of companionship, of familial contact, of the rituals and habits that made up their lives suddenly removed, perceive already some new aspect to how exactly they belonged in this place? Or how they belonged with one another? I had said a lifetime of goodnights and goodbyes in that room, either side of the bar, but that evening each one had carried some intensity that marked it out as not quite of the normal order. These people, I thought, had seen each other every day for years. For many there was nothing as formal as an arrangement to meet, there was no prior contact, no phone calls, no scheduled times. They simply walked up the road and took their chances on the evening's company. Perhaps they came up past the pond, or from the little row of cottages opposite the doctor's surgery, perhaps they drove down from their big house below the ridge of hills and drove back when they'd had rather too much to drink, in the knowledge that there were no longer any police cars out patrolling the roads around the hills at night. And I could see in their faces as they said those gravid goodnights that they were wondering who they might never see again. For we believed at the time that the virus would construct its grief for more than one of us in the bar that night. The talk was of breweries and pubs and businesses going bust, of how people were to live, to pay mortgages and rents, pay staff and suppliers and debts. It was a heady mix of desperation and desire – the breaking down of things and the radical potential of that breaking down to reshape what would come in its place.

I recalled particularly the conversation of one person from that evening. He was a man called Pete Cooper who got in the pub just about every day, and who ran a drinks distribution company in the local town. It had always struck me that his name was almost too perfect for the owner of a firm that had evolved out of what had once been the village brewery. The company had grown considerably over the hundred or so years it had been going but it was Pete's family who had always owned it. That night I could see in real time, in emotions that played out across his face as he talked about it, as yet another problem or pitfall crossed his mind, the realisation that all he had come to know might be about to end, right there and then. The material things so familiar to him as a child when his father had the business, the things he had enjoyed as a young man when he worked for his father, and now the things he worried over and saw as his achievements as the director, as the employer of two of his own children – the buildings, the pubs, the golf days, the landlords and landladies, the offices, the friendships, the standing he had come to enjoy in the area. The meaning he ascribed to himself. That evening his face had a haunted quality, but the cause was not simply the knowledge of coming change, or coming hardship – it was a deep uprooting which had affected him and in his eyes, which were the soft eyes of a man who bore so little anger or ill will to the world, I could see the utter shock of what had once been thought of as so certain turn out to be so fragile and easily and quickly undone. I thought of him again that day, sitting as I was now, quite alone, and for some reason what I recalled was his ability, honed from his schooldays so he told people, to capture exactly the likeness of other people's voices and mannerisms, and how he could impersonate almost anyone within an hour or so in their company. And I thought of how he had never used that skill with any malice in all the time that I had known him, and how it had made us laugh in that very room, a few

of us sat around the bar on a quiet night, enjoying
that peculiarly settled, restful feeling that came with
the golden hour of the daily regulars and Pete doing
someone off the telly, or the old man, or even me.

*   *   *   *

Somehow, some week, some day, it became a Friday
again. A bank holiday. The previous year the
government had announced they would move the
early May bank holiday from the 4th to the 8th, to
honour the 75th anniversary of VE Day. Of course
an extra public holiday could not be found. I don't
suppose they'd anticipated back then that they would
have a whole chunk of the population sat around
in a perpetual state of bank holiday by the time
the date rolled round. One morning I read that the
chancellor was worried people had become 'addicted'
to the financial support the government had provided
while people were prevented from going to work.
I would have asked him, if it came to it, to check
with the aristocratic class that he was so apparently
enamoured of about the nature of such addictions.
They seemed to have found it hard to wean themselves
off state aid for the last thousand or so years. I cannot
remember exactly when, but in the days following the
start of the lockdown we received a letter through the
front door telling us of plans to get the whole street
out of their houses and out on their front lawns and
doorsteps in order to toast the sacrifices made in the

war effort. The planned street parties may have had to be pared back somewhat, but the disease would simply not be allowed to defeat the communal efforts to memorialise the historic dead.

This sort of thing always made me think of my grandfather and his experiences in the war. Perhaps the village as I have so far described it does not immediately suggest itself as the kind of place to have a council estate. But there was one, at the south-eastern corner, built on what was once farmland belonging to the great house at Halton. My grandfather had lived his whole life up there, apart from his time at sea during the war. He told me once he had joined up to travel as much as anything, there being no other way for someone like him to see anything much of the world. Straight back here afterwards and a job for life with the gas board. It was always hard for me to picture him as a military man. I saw him forever as I used to out on the allotment. Blue jeans and a faded blue sweatshirt, stood resting one arm on his spade and rubbing his thumb and finger over his top lip where for most of his life, the navy aside of course, he'd grown a moustache. He was too old for the plot by now, and his much younger brother and one of my cousins looked after his twenty poles of flinty clay.

A few summers ago, my father organised an open mic in the pub on the May Day bank holiday. There were a few locals who brought their acoustic guitars down, and a couple of musician friends of my old man's even came out from London. A man called Monkey Wrench Mark (a hippieish conspiracy theorist whose deeply held antagonism to the accoutrements of 'progress' had resulted, long ago, in my father's nickname for him – a name that was a nod to the American author Edward Abbey's famous book about a group of environmental protesters turned saboteurs) who used the pub almost every day, got up to sing. Monkey Wrench Mark was born in Singapore, to Sri Lankan parents, and had lived in the village for twenty or so years. He moved here when he was working for the rail network. He lived alone now, his grown-up children having left home, and he spent his time walking in the hills and at home reading up on the various murky critiques of globalised capitalism and industrial environmental destruction that made up most of his conversation. He was a cheerful presence around the place and very much liked. That afternoon, if I remember it correctly, he was singing the Hank Williams standard 'Jambalaya' with no accompaniment, his regular turn, when an old woman shouted something like get that bloody ape off the stage. A younger woman who lived a few doors down from the pub at the time asked what she'd just said and was told to shut up and mind her own business by a large middle-aged man who was stood nearby. The man had a kind of ponytail, the last of his hair pulled back tightly over his head and tied up at the nape of his neck. He wore an old rugby top tucked into a pair of pale jeans. The younger woman told him to fuck off. The man looked temporarily defeated. Who are you anyway, he said. Are you even from here? I've not seen you here before. Where do you live? Where are you from? The young woman told him to keep his pet racist on her lead if she couldn't behave. She said it didn't matter where she was from. I'll tell you what matters, the man said, what matters is that *they* are bombing our boys. Or didn't she care about that? And while they are bombing our boys, he carried on, we're going to say what we like. I was sitting at the bar a few yards away and watching the incident. I nearly laughed in the man's face. Nearly. Nearly. Monkey Wrench Mark wore a white poppy on his battered old wax jacket, he would talk with anyone about the value of peace, about the destructive capacity of war and violence. He loved the wild flowers and orchids of his hills. I remembered how I had once been asked round to Mark's house after meeting him by chance while I was out walking. It had been like entering a kind of small, deconstructed library, an eccentric research centre for non-violent protest, post-9/11 truth theories and anti-war activism. There were books on every spare surface and more thrown across the sofa in the front room, there were piles of them on the floor next to the coffee table. On the kitchen table sat a large PC and a printer, and there were printed-off pages in small piles on top of chairs, on top of the stacks of books and magazines, and here and there on the floor. Some stapled together, some clipped, some loose. Mark claimed he knew exactly what and where it all was. It was all archived in a specific and quite natural way, in such a way in fact that he could lay his hand on any document he required at any moment. It was all material he'd culled from his regular sources. From websites like Architects & Engineers for 9/11 Truth, The Skeptic's Dictionary and The Daily Grail. He printed the material out in case anything should happen to his computer, or to the broadband in the area. He said this to me with a dark look in his eyes. No machine, for Mark, however useful, could be completely trusted. Next to the PC there was a stash of crosswords he'd cut out from the papers we took in the pub. He carried a few around with him whenever he went out, in case he needed stimulation in a pub, or under a tree, or wherever he might have chosen to stop for a rest. We drank tea.

That day my father had asked the man with the ponytail to leave the pub and later that night he wore the weary look he always did after there had been trouble of some kind. It was a sad look, and it had grown sadder the older he'd become. There was very little anger in him and he had a natural way of dealing with those situations without inflaming them. But sometimes I got the feeling he believed that certain important things had not been said. Not been done. We never saw the man back in the Lantern again. The younger woman and her husband moved away a little while afterwards. Somewhere we can get a bit more for our money, she'd told me. It was a shame that she left I thought, not, of course, that I had spoken to her very much or very often.

Every now and then Mark would get good and drunk and when he did he would ask very politely if those of us that were in the bar would object if he gave us a song. Of course, we would all say that we'd love to hear him, and he would sing 'Jambalaya' or 'King of the Road'. His singing, and his desire to sing, always functioned as his own cue to leave – to put his bag back over his shoulder and take his walking stick, decorated at the top with a bunch of coloured elastic bands and a jay's feather, from by the fire and take himself back across the fields to his home.

* * * *

The morning after the bank holiday, with its modified, muted VE Day celebrations, its raised glasses of rosé and awkward, distanced, half-remembered socialisation, came on with a violent reminder of the old reality of this pub, of me, of my life – I sat in the sun and tried the best I could to sweat a terrifying hangover out. It was a horror that seemed, after weeks without the kind of physiological trauma to which I might have once been at least a little inured, barely credible. The previous day had been a clement one and people all down the road had come out of

their houses to talk a little and to take a drink. For
one or two it was the first they'd seen of another
person in weeks. There had been music on the square
outside the shops and a few doors down from the
pub the man with the PA system, who in the normal
course of things would have set himself and his covers
band up in the beer garden of the Railway Arms
for the whole bank holiday weekend, was packing
his kit down. Perhaps there was just a little hint
of something unsaid in his wave that morning. A
sheepish acknowledgement that we had all enacted
some communal transgression of the rules. He was
wearing shorts and a pink Ralph Lauren polo shirt.
The rather sorry fake RAF uniform of the previous
day was presumably back in its box, or wherever it
was kept between bouts of fancy-dress nostalgia. The
whole scene was heavy with the poetry of our local
version of human decline – spoken in a language that
was both self-congratulatory and obsolete. On the
picnic table in front of me was an empty coffee cup.
By the back gate the recycling box was full of beer and
gin bottles. Opposite, the little row of cottages – red,
white and blue bunting, brick and flint, thatch. Union
flags wilting in the early sun. Blackbird and goldfinch
and great tit song regained their ascendant position
in the music of the place. Now that's what I call a
suburban bird-feeder. The old World War songs had
died out overnight. The woods up on the hills were
soundtracked by blackcap, song thrush, wood warbler,
chiffchaff. The open fields threw up their skylarks,

though not, it was true, in the number that they used
to, that they might do.

In his book *Desert Solitaire*, Edward Abbey
described a May Day morning in the Arizona badlands.
He raised a red rag alongside his Chinese windbells
and afterwards hoisted the Stars and Stripes.
He wrote how his gesture marked a balance on his
part, a desire for good fortune, good swill as he called
it, all round. Or the opposite – damnation for all.
I understood his sentiment, and felt for his hedged
bets against both revolution and his beloved flag –
I'd spent much of the previous day hedging bets of my
own, cheering when required to do so, clinking glasses,
privately muttering my doubts about the whole
performance. I was more in line with the damnation
aspect of Abbey's sentiments these days, though the
swill he mentioned felt about right for all of us out
here in the Home Counties – the pigs in charge of our
own trough. I found it harder and harder to summon
the will to argue for anything, were arguments even
available to me. I read almost constantly – the various
positions being taken online, people arguing about
how best to live, how to protect each other. The whole
process looked empty to me, in those days of our
solitudes. Perhaps the forced isolation had denuded my
faith in communal endeavour. Or perhaps my belief
in such things was always tenuous, stretched thin by
the evidence I had seen almost daily living in a place
like this, where the divergence between sections of

the community played out in a dismissive look here, a derisive comment there. Defensiveness, gossip, squabbles. Who was invited to what and with whom, the petty politics of social media and social standing. This place was plump with the self-satisfaction of the wealthy, the well fed, the winners, and yet bloodied with small-town violence and muddied with ordinary labour. There were all the everyday eccentricities of people anywhere and so it was that you might feel profound tenderness for the place one minute and despise it the next. Perhaps this ambivalence is why I could no longer argue for anything, could no longer feel that singular sense of things as meaning one thing and one thing only. Perhaps this is why I could never leave.

The news media continued to talk to itself, the empty chamber in Parliament a symbol of something forcing itself through the last of the motions, while everywhere else people relearned how they might want things to be, turned inward or turned off the news, heeded or ignored the advice, threw their various cautions to the wind. Some days, however, the real world pressed itself hard upon me. The physical world of the earth itself. A couple of years ago, I took on a plot down at the allotments from an old family friend. As with most things, my initial motivation was almost purely one of affectation. The whole thing seemed congruent with the styling of myself as the local poet, as namer of the birds and the trees, as man of the region. Perhaps it coincided with the reading jag I was on back then.

Edward Abbey, Wendell Berry. Some thoughts from
Berry's essay 'Think Little' had long stayed with me,
I knew that much, thoughts in which Berry described
how transformative it was for anyone to undertake the
task of looking after a little bit of earth, to protect its
soil, to replenish, to offer as well as to extract. However
it began, I was thankful for the growing of things now.
And I had come to understand the time on my little
plot as a further complication of my received ideas
of work. After a few hours digging, for example, the
ground had been worked over. I had been put to work
– things, done properly, could be said to have been
working well. And yet I felt something almost defiantly
at odds with my feelings towards waged work. This
was non-transactional time. It was something I did,
but not, somehow, something that I *was* in the eyes of
others. It felt like a rejection of the way I understood so
many of us living here, all jostling for self-identifiable
position, exchanging and updating statuses, one for
another. Money, power, prestige, comfort. The materiel
in these skirmishes was house prices, expensive
bicycles, moral superiority. The arms race of the school
gate. And then there was the soft power that came
with the prestige of the arts. The self-proclaimed
'creatives' of the village, with the violence that their
newly coined noun had done at the altar of the
adjective. I do not wish to downplay my own collusion
in all this. The local poet, the bore, the big mouth. The
allotment and the long walks, begun as affectation,
fertiliser for my own sense of self and worth. I brought

my own sacrifices to the festival of the fake, of the phony along with all the others.

The soil was a text of its own, an essay on the gone seasons and old sun and past life become mulch. It was specific. Edward Abbey talked of his desire, in heading to the desert, to absent himself from those aspects of his own culture he had come to see as repellant, as distracting, as, on a deep level, perhaps even untrue. He was rejecting the Kantian, the description and categorisation of the human, the scientific. He was attempting to re-enter the world, to once again be alive within it. This was how it felt to me, planting a specific, individual bean plant, the seeds of which I had been given by my grandfather, dried from his own stock, without recourse to horticultural study, to varieties, to Latin names – those categories which ultimately gave way to hierarchies. It was unqualified, profligate life, and all its own at that, this small thing making and remaking itself in the soil. I walked across the ground, between the distinct patches of bare earth and their plants, their discrete, rickety, knocked-together shacks and greenhouses, their netting and fencing, their tools and clods and tilth, the pile of manure in the middle of the plot, people bending towards soil in which they had invested so hard and so well. It was more profound than ownership, this way with the land. Back when I had the will, I would every now and then try to suggest to fellow allotment holders like Pete the Pole, a local scaffolder who drank in The Paper Lantern, that he was involved in an intimate, radical act when he undertook the work required of him on his plot, but my arguments never quite washed. It's just fresh veg, you daft trot, he would say. Now I would simply join in the easy, practical conversation of those of us with a few poles of our own. I had given up on theory, on politics, when applied to the ground beneath us. In the pub our little patches were a shortcut into talk that was both flippant and deeply felt. The status symbols of so much village life – the jobs, the schools, the huge and brutal cars, seemed meaningless when the talk turned to digging and timings and tender plants. That morning there was work to be done, hangover or no.

I walked to the plot via a long, wide street lined with plane trees and hornbeam, which ran north and parallel to the main road out of the village towards the town. The houses on this road were the most desirable addresses in the village. The front drives were full of statement cars and in the previous decade or so any nod to old-fashioned cottage garden planting had made way for the monoculture of lawns and gravel. A backdrop for the spotless Range Rovers, BMWs and Jeeps. A boulevard monument to petroleum and the global motor trade. About halfway down the length of the road and making the corner with one of the streets that ran down to the main road out of the village was a large house with a For Sale sign in the front garden. This house would perhaps not suggest anything much as you walked past – it was an attractive white building with a gabled roof, its timber frame painted white along with its brickwork. It wasn't so much that I always made note of it, more that as I passed by I was put in mind of things from the well of my own memory. Not of the house, which I had never so much as set foot in, but of my friend Stephen, the person who first told me of the scientist Cecilia Payne-Gaposchkin, and of the fact that she had once lived in this house. In her own lifetime, she was renowned as an eminent astronomer, and being born in 1900, that rather inevitably came with the usual qualifications – the greatest *woman* astronomer of her time, a remarkable *female* scientist. Stories of her work being obscured, her discoveries claimed elsewhere. The usual tawdry, despicable stuff. Stephen took a great deal of pleasure in the fact that a scientist of real note had lived here in the village, and I took pleasure in the fact that his own career in some, albeit loose way echoed hers through time. In the local library they kept a number of copies of Payne-Gaposchkin's autobiography. In the first chapter she described the 'pagan' heritage of her name and the fact that there had been people bearing the name Payne at the foot of these hills since long before the Romans arrived. It was the passage after that which I had always found so compelling. Writing of her family history, she described herself as somehow beyond being what she saw as a simple idea of

English – she described an international spirit, a
compulsion to not just see the world, but to belong to
it that ranged beyond borders. A German mother, a
Russian husband, a Greek son-in-law. As I remember
it now, when I first read that book, at Stephen's
house in the chair that stood by the bookcase in the
dining room, I was struck by the sense of belonging
she could distil in the Buckinghamshire soil, the
same soil I had begun, then, to feel so strongly about,
and yet she could look with such generosity at the
rest of the world. Here was an attachment to the
place that didn't come with the attendant jingoism
I encountered time and again. It was a complicated,
worldly love. In her book she writes of the complexity
of that love, tending away from the reactionary, away
from the simplistic. Even remembered now, long after
the words first affected me, I recall how that first
passage of the book seemed even more suggestive
to me, even more profound, than her description of
finding a bee orchid in the garden of that house in the
village and how that single plant changed the course
of her life, and the garden became her incipient
scientific training ground.

And so I walked past the house most mornings,
noted the small plaque above the front door and
thought of Cecilia in the observatory at Harvard or
the labs at Cambridge. Of the passage at the end of
her book when she describes the social frustrations
of her early life, the prioritising of her brother's

education, her inability to dance or talk to boys, her
lack of opportunity in English scientific circles. It
was a wonder to me how all this, and more of my own
memories that had become somehow connected, came
to mind simply by walking past a building. At the
north end of the road a little dirt track ran around the
back of a row of houses and down to the allotments.
That morning the path was coddled in beech leaves
and nettles, the first of the cow parsley.

On my patch I watered and earthed up the potatoes
and sowed a couple of rows of spinach. The ground was
dry and dusty. Over a period of just a few weeks it had
turned a dull grey where in the thick of winter it was
a rich brown. I saw my grandfather on his patch a few
plots down and stopped to say hello. He warned of a
frost in the next few nights. Don't risk anything tender
yet, he told me. I couldn't help notice the beauty of
his sentence, its poise, the seed-like quality of hope it
communicated. I finished my tasks, cleaned up and
locked the shed.

From the allotments I crossed the main road and
headed east towards the canal, down another track
of white chalk and flint, ran past a large park and
then into a thin, hedge-lined lane. The lane here
was the kind of half-hidden place where tradition
dictated teenagers attend to their first kisses and
perhaps even their initial sticky fumblings. If I
thought back now to that age it struck me that here

even those ecstatic, innocent moments were already, at twelve or thirteen, loaded with the weight and shame of status. Here where children were sieved through a selection process for secondary school, where they were ascribed at that moment a type, a category – and with that attendant modes of thought and behaviour – they found perhaps that individual desires must early on be subsumed for the sake of propriety. Girls or boys from one school or the other did certain things the others did not. Sex should not be a loss of innocence, but a reclamation of it. An act of unalloyed, omnivorous living. The plants, I thought that morning, perhaps understood this better than all things.

The canal towpath led out of the village and across the county to the east. After ten miles or so the water in this arm of the canal petered out, the bed running dry at the edge of a large field. There the bottom of the canal bed was already, even this early in the year, dried to an almost pure white. Huge cracks had opened up in the hardened chalk. We had experienced by then two months with next to no rainfall. The earth opened up like a sore, the chalk streams disappeared into the ground. On top of everything – the virus, the daily death toll, the loneliness, the hangover – every day we walked confronted by the evidence of our great failure, our true fallibility: we were apparently incapable of husbanding the planet we lived on and lived off. Even here, where the hammer fell least hard, there was, if you cared to look, the detritus and the signage of our terminally degraded world.

Our section, our arm, was a small feeder of the Grand Union Canal, and you could, if you chose to, or had the time, walk the towpath from the village all the way to London. The arm had only ever been navigable for a short while, hamstrung as it had been by constant leaks. A canal that leaked – there was something so perfectly pathetic about it. Fitting for a place that seemed now so at odds with the true nature of the world that its works failed under the strain of their own element. A place that had bastardised the very features of the earth that had given it a name, that had broken them, spent them, ruined them for the sake of servitude, progress, industry and wealth.

At a narrow point where the boats would have once unloaded their cargo – mostly destined for the big manor house on the edge of the village – there was now a bench. I sat and watched and listened. Swifts overhead in yet another huge blue sky, swallows taking their food from a midge hatch on the surface. It was still devoid of any human noise in those early mornings, though we had begun to notice a few more cars on the roads. A new point of discussion in the pharmacy queue. Little changes to the human world, mirroring the incremental growth that marked the seasons, the new birds arriving. The big house here had been built by a prominent family in the local area. In fact, a prominent family worldwide. A family which had once boasted the largest private fortune in the world, and had produced bankers, winemakers, property owners. The name was still well known. They had once owned vast amounts of land in the area, had built big, ostentatious houses across the county. There were pubs to which the family had given their name. There were photographs in the local museum of them having their carriages pulled through town not by horses, but by a team of zebras. There were stories of the wild animals they once kept in their private collection – escapees and dangerous exotics.

A plastic bag full of dog shit hung from a tree along the path. Dog shit was a fact of the towpath, of the bushes, the grass, the beer garden of the pub. I thought of all the dogs of The Paper Lantern, the cockapoos and miniature schnauzers, the terriers and collies. Big Pete's Weimaraner. These were the collected specimens of our time. In places like this, our dogs had outgrown their old categories of work and become archetypal, tarotic. They stood now for human loneliness and all its opposites and inversions, for the warm breath of something living alongside you. The same thing the pub had come to mean in its closure – companionship. At one time in my life I had grown to feel a strong dislike of the animals. Not the unease of childhood fear, but a more pungent antipathy. It was no fault of their own, of course, I had simply once had an idea for a sequence of poems about them which I later discovered the German poet Durs Grünbein had already written. His poem could not be improved upon and so the animals themselves became yet another symbol of my own many failures. But now I had come to believe in them, if not like them, and their little bags, left on the waypaths of the county, were like offerings to a long-forgotten or as yet unnamed god. I believed in all these signs now, signs of the damage being done by a fanaticism just as irrational, as wild and as fervid as any of the religious or political bogeymen the media continued to drag in front of us, and one based on a fallacy just as fantastical as that of a benevolent supernatural being – that of infinite and perpetual economic growth. I thought of the history of all the money and property and goods that had made their way past where I was now sitting and on up to the big house. How international it felt to me, to imagine the tropical plants in the gardens, the exotic animals, the global finance, politics, wars. And how shrunken it now felt, this little wood and little bench on an unremarkable stretch of disused canal. The spent grandeur that had become nothing more than an insular little town full of dogs and dog shit and failed ambitions like my own. The rubbish in the hedgerows, the fly-tipped waste in the lay-bys on the way to the towns, dark rubber marks on the roads, patches of spilled oil. The Deep Mill Diner, closed and shuttered up for years out on the London road. For Sale signs. Roadkill muntjac, roadkill badger. Abandoned petrol stations. Kill your speed. Roadkill pheasant, roadkill fox. Chalk House (in the Arts and Crafts style). The Cock and Rabbit, home-cooked food, live music, real ales. Single-track road. Jackdaw. Buzzard. The Firecrest, 2 Courses for £15. No HS2 – No business case. No environmental case. No case at all. Luxury retirement village. Builders' merchants. High Speed Two Works Exit. Here were the signs of the true orthodoxy, everywhere you cared to look. Waste and litter was all we were good for. Feckless, endless consumption and its detritus – that was the way of things now for the people of this country and the dogs that walked beside them.

* * * *

Perhaps The Paper Lantern itself – this suddenly strange, suddenly useless and rather sad-looking building just off the main street in our unimportant village – could bear a little description. Where to start. Perhaps with the plain, greyish front door on South Street, which was also the road out of the place, the road to the big city and all that might once have meant. Upon entry, that door led to two bars, one to the left and another to the right. Mostly the building was seventeenth century, half-timber, two-storeyed and with a good-sized garden. Through the bar on your right-hand side lay another small room, until recently a kind of modest dining room favoured by the more elderly customers, but now, its chairs up

on the tables and empty of custom, it functioned as
a kind of utility room for the three of us remaining.
It had become home to a pair of bicycles my parents
had begun to use again for the first time in years, a
clothes horse, a couple of bags of old clothes they had
culled over the past few weeks in various periods of
organisation. The bags were a sacrifice, a pruning,
they were the symbols of a refreshed way of being.
Of, perhaps, a new material sobriety. The news hinted
at the possibility of an emergent culture across the
country. Exercise, the outdoors, birdsong. Less traffic,
less ostentatious travel. Wardrobes had been thinned
along with expectations. All things were being held to
various kinds of account.

Between the dining room and the saloon bar, as we
called it, was a small window framed in a little nook
under the stairwell that led up to the living quarters
of the pub. Up to my own rather sorry little room.
Through this glass pane you could look down into
the old cellar, and above it there was a small plaque
displaying a couple of bits of village folklore of the
kind that I am sure any resident of any comparable
village or town would find utterly unremarkable.
Here was the story that the cellar had access to a
series of tunnels that linked The Paper Lantern to
the larger White Horse Hotel on the high street, and
that in fact there were also tunnels leading to the
church away across the fields to the south of the pub.
The tunnels' purposes were as dubious as the truth

of the architecture itself – none had ever been found, either for use in shuttling prostitutes along from the Lantern (which, if the stories were to be believed, it seemed had always offered something with a little more piquancy than the more expensive, and in those days at least, more homogenous fare on offer at the brewery-pub establishments on the high street proper) to the White Horse in its coaching-house days, or, either more or less innocently, to carry a beer barrel or two down to the church. The regulars told these stories to new visitors now and then, eyebrows arched, voices tinged with something half-hearted, or perhaps light-hearted, in the telling. They would show them the stone that sat outside the front door, and its apparently ancient hand-carved female equivalent of the school-desk classic cock-and-balls. In fine, deliberate lines the stone showed, through a kind of trigonometric symbolism, exactly what was once, supposedly, available at the Lantern that wasn't elsewhere.

The bar on the left as you entered was colloquially known as the sports bar, but the presence of a TV on the far wall was the only concession to what might be accurately called sport. This same room had once housed the very first television set to be found anywhere in the village, purchased and installed in the bar for the purpose of allowing the customers to watch Eric Boon fight Arthur Danahar in the first televised boxing match. I thought of how the habits

of different generations recall themselves across time
in spaces like this. How many drinks had been taken,
how many games of football had been watched, how
many arguments started and settled. For our part,
we provided a darts board, cards from behind the bar,
and an antique-looking game called Tripletell which
I had never seen anywhere else. The game involved
a small pool cue and cue ball and a long thin wooden
frame marked by a series of sections of diminishing
sizes. Each section had a points value, finally reaching
20, which was both the smallest section and the
furthest from the bottom of the frame. The object of
the game was to play the cue ball up the frame, which
was slightly inclined, until it stopped in the small
metal gates that marked each section. There was a
scoring system of first-to-100, though you had to finish
on exactly 100, anything over causing the player to
go bust in much the same way as a finish in darts.
Sunday nights used to be Tripletell nights, when we
would put the frame out on a table in the back room
and Jim and Tom, two of the pub's younger regulars,
both in their mid-twenties and lashed to the village
by some kind of inertia of their own, would play for
pennies. Seemingly unique among their peers, these
two young men were apparently immune to the pull
of the capital, or the university towns, which, after
years and years of pushing the virtues of bigger, more
cultural, more exciting elsewheres, of selling the scam
of higher education that was so ubiquitous as to be
both worthless and inevitable and finally, cripplingly

expensive, had for the most part emptied the area
of people their age. Another loss to tot up at the bar
alongside the forgotten industries, the lace-making
and the flint-quarrying and duck-breeding, the local
accent, multitude of insects, certain species of birds
– cuckoos, nightingales, corn buntings – and healthy,
clear chalk streams.

In the days before all this solitude you could rely on
finding one of the Petes we all called Pete the Pecker
'at home' as he would say, in the sports bar, stood
by the hatch which opened from behind the bar for
the staff to get out and clear glasses or collect plates.
Pete's family lived in a small cottage up the hill to the
south of the village. An old flint and brick building
in a little row that ran along a track towards an old
manor house. He would tell you that his surname
was specifically local, attached to the village since
at least the sixteenth century. His name, he would
say, was even older than his house. I was a few years
younger than him, but remembered him from the
grammar school in the nearby town. The school that
had created its arms race of private tuition and extra
classes and in my experience no small number of lost
souls like Andy, who couldn't quite seem to reconcile
how the world had never offered up its wonders to
them, having been told almost daily from the age of
eleven to eighteen that this was their destiny. One of
the gifted. The top whatever percentile of intellects
in the country. The school went on selling itself to its

pupils long after they'd begun their instruction. No doubt the kids were mostly smart investments. But a few, like Pete, emerged from those days of Latin and quadrangles, of heavily funded school sports, of the camaraderie and the casual homophobia only an all-boys school can engender, and found themselves in a world that was harder than they thought it ought to be. A world, it turned out, that didn't care nearly as much as they thought about their actually rather second-rate schooling. They might meet somebody genuinely aristocratic, or properly rich, or talented, or educated at that next, even more 'selective' level, and their expectations of a gilded life met the grubby reality. Perhaps they dropped out of university, finding that they didn't fit in with the same ease they did at school. Perhaps their jokes no longer landed. The 'gay' stuff didn't wash, the bluster didn't quite come over. They were just one of any number of middling students of English literature, say. It turned out that many more people than might have been supposed had read Bukowski, the Beats, Burgess, Ballard. They weren't as interesting or original as they imagined. They came back to the village after that disastrous first year, they got a job for a local building company and for that first summer everything turned great again. Their gang from school were all back, they had a bit of money. They drank in the Lantern every night and on the weekends they went into the town. On the site they were once more the great talker,

the thinker, the joker. They had read the books, and
they made everybody laugh in the pub after work
on a Friday afternoon. Slowly it all accumulated
into something like a self. The heroic autodidact. No
university for them but instead the world of work
and a little reading. They knew a little more than a
little bit about almost everything. Football, motor
racing, cricket, rugby, boxing. They were especially
pleased with themselves to show off their knowledge
of boxing. Politics, of course, local history, etymology.
They were the first person Monkey Wrench Mark took
his crossword to when he'd got as far as he could. In
places like The Paper Lantern they were always at
home. Was any of this Pete's life though? I couldn't
truthfully say. Sometimes it was as if I had forgotten
which bits of which history were his and which were
mine, which were fact and which were fear, which
had come to pass and which were the accumulation
of my own anxious imagination. Was it not the truth
that I had in fact myself gone off to university and
lasted no more than a couple of weeks before coming
home, disappointed with what I found in the world
outside the village and in myself. Or had I avoided it
altogether, worried as I undoubtedly was about being
found out as the fraud I knew myself to be.

Pete the Pecker had come to feel so at home here
in the pub, in fact, that a packed sports bar once
provided him with an audience as he performed the
astonishing feat of becoming visibly aroused during

his own rendition of Nick Drake's 'Pink Moon' at one
of the pub's open mic nights. Six foot five, twenty
stone and with his best friend Adam playing the song
quite beautifully sitting just behind him, and as that
soft, otherworldly melody passed from Pete to his
audience across the room, we watched a quite obvious
erection slowly stir and announce itself through his
dark blue tracksuit bottoms. Pete didn't seem to
notice, or perhaps didn't care. He had drifted away
with the song, with its odd phrasing and its dreamlike
chord progression and the doleful melancholic power
its lyrics had on him. Poetry, one supposes. I don't
remember anybody bringing it up with him after he'd
finished and gone back to his place at the bar. I don't
remember anyone ever bringing it up.

In the emptiness and disuse of the previous weeks,
the pub had settled into a novel sort of disorder.
The trays of crisps sat up on the bar in the saloon
alongside newspapers, cleaning products, now
and then a coffee cup or a mobile phone. The place
was a perpetual Sunday morning. The tall tables
by the windows provided a spot for seedlings and
propagation trays. There were gaps in the spirits
behind the bar where rum and bourbon bottles used
to stand. Each week Friday teatime passed without
the teachers overrunning the sports bar, without
the regulars in the saloon, the cyclists and families
and dogs in the beer garden. After a lifetime of
imagining, of thinking and dreaming it up, this is

what eventually passed for my truly dropping out –
an absence of individual, specific people, which turned
into an absence of the times they were associated
with, which became an absence of time altogether.
Time had become simply the choreography of my and
my mother and father's days, surrounded everywhere
by monuments to its once true function. Or by
memory, going off like the beer in the cold store,
forgetting itself in the dementia of becoming the past,
obsolete, meaningless.

* * * *

The field directly to the south of the pub, and the
road that ran between the two, were both named
The Witchell, and in any other summer the field would
be serving as the village cricket club's second ground.
Training for the youngsters, colts and pub games, that
sort of thing. A small path led around the field along its
eastern edge and down past a large pond towards the
church. Another piece of local folklore and a common
pub story told that the field took its name from the time
when the church was first being built. The villagers
laid the foundations in this field, brought the stone
and flint and timber to build with, but the morning
after their first day's work, they arrived back at the
site to find that during the night everything had been
moved a couple of fields south. The local fairies and
witches, so the story went, had long since claimed this
particular piece of ground for their own, and when the

same thing happened a few days and nights in a row, the people gave up and the church was eventually built in its present location. Rumours of witches and witchcraft continued to attach themselves to the field, and there was a fourteenth-century reference to it as the 'Wychewelle Croft'. More prosaic and so, of course, much more likely, was that the village had moved further to the north in order to expand into its status as a market town, to move closer to the drover's road that had by now become the high street. Commerce and expansion, the slow turning away from the folkloric, the superstitious. The drift, that started even before the assizes and markets and little flint churches and bells built by Ellis Knight, and families like de Gournay and de Fiennes, even before this place was known by its other, older names – Gloversacre, Oxpennyng, Northbrech, le Maline, Socchfeld, Medecroft, Paradise – the drift from the house of the spirit to the house of finance. The slippery and mutable definitions of space, of human demarcations which were really demarcations of time. One history of this place, the one that could be read in the archives, was that which told of these names and manors, of tithes and rents. Of boundaries prone to be moved, and with them whole settlements. Which was not to say, of course, that the church itself hadn't always represented both the house of the spirit and the house of the pound in equal measure. In fact, this church had its own special place in the entwined histories of money and the soul, in the double nature of the word 'salvation' – the country's first ever penny savings bank was formed there in the vestry. In this very place where money and morality still most subtly synthesise themselves. Give me the witches and fairies that shift bricks and stone and flint and timber overnight. Not here, they say. Not now.

* * * *

Little rituals filled the days. Walking, filling the coffee machine, counting ice cubes into my glass, the two-and-a-half-second glug of spirit, even my note-taking, the naming of things. Take a day at random – nuthatch, great tit, blue tit, greenfinch, meadow pipit, thrush, kestrel, kite, kite, kite, rook, pheasant, wood pigeon. The names, though, did not tell of them well enough. Words had diminished them into nothingness. Look how they die when I turn them into marks on the page.

* * * *

Lonely, fraught, uncanny days. I was up at four with the sun and the birdsong. My days had taken on some of the rhythm of these non-human things, beginning in the dim first light and settling into the long lull of the afternoon before a brief flare of energy as the evening turned into the night. My walks began at dawn now, avoiding the increased traffic along the towpath, in the woods, on the hills. Up at the Boer War Memorial that stood at the highest point of Coombe Hill people appeared to be luxuriating in a new faculty for time, space. The car park at the top overspilled most days now. The rigidity of weekends, weekdays, working hours all somehow eroded. By late afternoon the grassy hilltop surrounding the austere spike memorialising yet more of the dead was littered with beer cans and crisp packets, plastic bottles, clingfilm. More dog shit. Even at our lowest point we could find it in ourselves to desecrate the earth. One afternoon my mother took a couple of recycling bags up the hill and cleared up a bit. She brought a few sacks of rubbish down and put them in the pub bins. From the top of the hill I took in the view across the vale and out over a landscape of farmland and small settlements, four counties on a clear day, the field below and to the east with its growing little community of Portaloos, trucks and vans all beginning the first visible stages of the work being done on the new high-speed railway that was to run across the scarp alongside the village. This vast national project known to everyone by its abbreviation of HS2 would, so we were told, join London to the cities in the north while also allowing fast, easy travel to the continent. The project had been discussed for a few years and become mired in public anger, the projected route destined to destroy tracts of ancient woodland, to utterly remake the countryside in places similar to ours the whole length of the country. At one level, from what could reasonably be gleaned from the news, the whole thing had become a bloated and expensive mess, on another it had the effect of arousing a kind of folk anger. This was something with meaning beyond the old faultlines of party politics, or the still palpable class structures that underpinned our place. Everybody here had long since made up their mind that the line was going to destroy the village as they knew it, and beyond that affect each of them in their own discrete ways. It might well have been the case that the train line was absolutely a necessity. Those who had doubts or misgivings might have been wrong to think of it as an expensive and overcomplicated mistake, an obliterating force in the landscape, shattering the woods and little towns and villages along its route. But there seemed to me to be something rotten in the soul of the thing. It was not simply a matter of the practicalities, of increased passenger numbers, of the easing of the burden on other routes, of reducing car use and facilitating access to the north. It goes without saying that this is the stuff that concerned most people, and rightly, I'm sure, but was there not also some aspect to the whole endeavour that operated on another plane? There was the profiteering, the thuggery, the mendaciousness, the corruption. This had all become so intrinsic to this country's business, to everything that the politicians and industrialists and planners and lobbyists got up to, that it felt impossible to get beyond it. There might well have been a case to be made for this railway line, or any other, and for the trees that needed to come down to make way, for the damage and degradation – I couldn't have said – but I knew for certain that there were people making money out of all the despoil. That there were motives at play beyond the infrastructural benefit to the nation. Nothing was ever done solely for the general good, not without some financial sluicing off going on at the same time. And so it came as no real surprise to find a project such as this one, which we were told was something to welcome, something being undertaken for our own good, had apparently hired a team of security guards, and had harassed and bullied anyone who protested against the work, or that the work sometimes went ahead without the necessary environmental surveys or licenses – and it was this element, this subtle note of easy brutality that caused the heart to sink. The rationale, good or bad, became a side point, a ridiculous irrelevance in fact, in the face of those unsavoury fragments of the truth.

I walked south, away from the monument along the Ridgeway and down the opposite side of the hill. Down through the beech woods, the bluebells and wild garlic by now just gone over from full flower to seed, the light modulated through the greenscale of the layers of beech leaves in the canopy. The odd ash, rowan, hawthorn. Woodpecker, blackcap, thrush, goldcrest. I totted up my little lists. I heard more than I saw. Down past the farm at the bottom of the wood, on the corner of the road that skirts the hill I took the footpath as it crossed the grounds at Chequers. Warnings about straying from the small track in the grass, CCTV cameras on the fenceposts. I took the path across the grounds and looked to my right over the large estate park, cleared of all but a dozen or so trees, a few sheep grazing the grass. Crows and rooks. Red kites. A single, languid buzzard.

Over the previous couple of weeks it had been hard not to think about the proximity of this place, of its purpose, its people. It occupied my thoughts, drew my eye. I found myself walking this way day after day and wondering if any of 'them' were here, what future was being imagined for us in those old rooms. A helicopter passed and I read it like augury. I took up positions relating to the place, attempts at parsing some meaning in the fact of the house being here, or perhaps just being. It was a monument of its own, of course. To the almost limitless accumulation of its associated class for two hundred, three hundred years. Perhaps more. To the complacency of power at best, to its callousness at worst. Either way, to the violence it seems always to carry in its wake. Displaced violence here, where all worldly truths were kept conveniently at arm's length.

Edward Abbey described the 'fondness' he believed the owl had for its prey, writing of something like affection between the owl and its rabbit before the kill. He wondered if the feeling was in some way reciprocated, if the rabbit felt, finally, some sense of peace or perhaps a kind of resolution with its status in its ultimate act of being eaten. As if the life of the rabbit was simply anxiety – the constant demand for food, for sex, for shelter, and so death, at the right talons, became a kind of resolution. The surface violence of the world seemed easy for Abbey to anthropomorphise despite his own instinct, or perhaps his desire, to avoid it. For him, the question was whether the rabbit felt a kind of love at the end. He did not want to talk of enemies, natural or otherwise, in a system he called well organised. I was unconvinced, now, by his argument. It relied too heavily on acquiescence to hierarchy, to the acceptance that what was, was well organised. Abbey betrayed his own wish to see the world as things beyond the bounds of taxonomy, of category. Surely the rabbit did not classify itself as 'prey', or even understand what was 'rabbit'. Words are our own special depreciation of the world. In Abbey's America at that moment, any façade of organisation, of order of any kind, looked like it was crumbling by the day. Generations of stratified violence, of the stacked cards of capital, of wealth – and the racism and injustice that were so enmeshed with it, that had in fact generated it – were once more working their way through society in the power structures that appeared ever more brutal, ever more sadistic. Peaceful protest, some quarters pleaded. As if they hadn't had that chance before and ignored it. Who could watch now and not want the rabbit, finally, to turn on the owl and burn his roost to the ground? Enough, the owl must come to understand. Enough.

I realised of course that I played my own part in the violence of my times, that I inherited the violence of all the years that preceded me. And we were perhaps, no better here than in America, certainly no less implicated, no more innocent. I looked down the hill at the brickwork of this eminent building that sometimes seemed to exult in its place here in the hills, and sometimes seemed sullen or sheepish, hidden in the service trees that surrounded it. The brick of that house was pointed with the blood and bone of the crimes of industrial exploitation, all its environmental and human ravages. In the act of parliament in which the house was gifted to the nation as the prime minister's country retreat, then-owner Sir Arthur Lee wrote that 'the better the health of our rulers the more sanely will they rule and the inducement to spend two days a week in the high and pure air of the Chiltern hills and woods will, it is hoped, benefit the nation as well as its chosen leaders.' I wondered if the building took its share of blame, too, when its malignant aspect appeared to be in the ascendant. It sat brooding at me that day while the government appeared to be abdicating any last semblance of reason. Guilt and shame bring their own sedimentary recriminations, of course, and the plain truth was that these walks were the least of my own indulgences. I was too eager to feel like this, to crow about my own inadequacies in order that they might count as conscience. Dormancy was our crime out here in England's well-fed middle – leafletting for the Labour Party or making coffee at the local Party's monthly reading group in the Lantern appeared to me then as pure posture, or worse, as acts

I might have simply imagined. Walking and reading were not enough, it occurred to me.

My reading matter in those days came from the shelves in the spare room in which I had, for some years now, found myself living. My own books remained packed up in boxes in the garage. A symbol of the hoped-for impermanence of the arrangement. But weeks had become months then years. The books on the shelves were my parents'. Their library of the American West. I reread Edward Abbey, Mary Austin, Gretel Ehrlich. Books I remembered from childhood and which had once created in me – along with their music, their films, their clothes – a strange and lasting longing for America. I desired its music, its literature, its food. But most keenly I wanted its vast and apparently wild spaces. For most people my age that might have meant travel, but for me that had always been impossible. I could only watch my generation's own colonial gestures, could only live them vicariously through my friends – the gap years and cheap international flights, the shrunken post-internet world, 'doing' South Asia, Africa, Australia, America – a new version of individuated grasping, the newly globalised world of the wealthy. The ironic gesture of its borders. I would have loved to see these places, but the thought of travel, even now, made me sick. So I stayed here when the exotic trips were taken, just as I did when the universities took my peers away, and then the city did, and then home-ownership, and

then children. I read and listened to records and made
do with my imagination. America was something I
read and heard and experienced through the other
channels of its culture. Coke and denim workwear,
skateboarding, the electric guitar. Dreams of mesas
and wide rivers and tall trees. Reading Abbey again
now I was struck by the sublime confidence with
which he walked through the land, a confidence that
read to me then as yet another colonial posture. My
friends from school had moved through the world with
the same sense, I think – they descended on markets
in foreign countries with the power to purchase, they
caroused in foreign cities knowing real danger was a
statistical anomaly. Strippers in Las Vegas, drugs in
the Balearics, the cheap, yet-to-be-spoiled paradises of
Thailand and Bali. All there for the consuming. Abbey
had on one hand a deep knowledge and connection
to his places, but on the other a too-easy disdain
for people unlike him, the innate sense of his own
primacy that almost without his noticing slipped into
racism and misogyny. At times I put the book down
and thought he was the perfect guide for those days
we now faced, that the mistakes we were still making
were in his tradition as well as the traditions he saw
as his adversaries' – the traditions of 'progress', of the
developer, of the market.

Having crossed the grounds at Chequers, I took the
path across a wide field. Here, in the early mornings
or late afternoons, skylarks – at times perceived only

59

as song, as a flute-like tone that burst, disembodied, birdless, from the blue – climbed in stages high into the clear sky, or descended back down into the grasses and their hidden nests. I stopped and recorded the song on my phone. I had long given up trying to photograph them. The song was enough. Enough for what, I thought to myself. I had nobody to play the recordings to. Perhaps I kept them for some far-off winter day. A hedged bet against another season.

At the western edge of the field, I entered a small wood, skirted its rim round to the north until, at the other side, I came through a gate into a suddenly quite different landscape. The beeches and oaks and ash were gone, and the hills themselves seemed smaller. The lush grassland was dotted everywhere with small, squat box trees, the white chalk path running up and over the hillocks that stretched ahead of me. Away to the north I could see Pulpit Hill and the deep, ancient, box wood that I would walk through on my way back. Very near here, when I was still at school, a group of kids a few years older began to host illegal parties in one of the hidden valleys just to the north-west. I never went but one or two friends of mine did. They renamed the place Happy Valley, or perhaps they took some older name that had fallen out of use and repurposed it. For a couple of years these parties went on, secret until the day itself, when word would spread and, after the pubs closed, people would take themselves off into the woods and listen to music

on the huge PA systems they had erected and dance
and take drugs. Dancing. Drugs. All that was always
beyond me somehow too. One of the organisers of
those old raves still came into the Lantern now and
then. I'd never known him as anything other than
V. I remember one occasion a few years ago when he
was sitting on his own in a little corner of the saloon
bar. The kitchen had closed so he proceeded to take
out a packet of salami and a loaf of bread. He didn't
ask, or seem to care if he'd been perceived to have
broken any kind of rule, or if he'd contravened some
delicate point of etiquette. He had just got out of
hospital, had damaged his cruciate ligaments playing
football, and his right leg had a brace around the
knee. I thought of him whenever I walked across this
section of hills. I remembered that on another occasion
he was asked not to take his medication at the bar.
It was around the same time and he was on heavy
prescription painkillers for his injury. My mother told
him she knew exactly what he was taking and that he
shouldn't leave the bottle on the bar next to his drink
and that he certainly should not be washing it down
with six pints of cider. She took his car keys off him
that night and insisted on calling a cab to take him
home. He used to tell one particular story over and
over again, which involved him going out clubbing
one night with a famous eighties pop singer and his
brother back when he was still putting on parties and
club nights. He said the singer's brother had spent
an hour or so telling him about the best cocaine he

had ever taken, which was, unsurprisingly, when
he had been touring with his brother in Colombia.
V said the singer's brother had gone on to instruct
him, in some detail, as to how one might make
something quite like the drug just using the leaf of
the coca plant and a microwave. Apparently, you
simply kept putting a tightly wrapped package of the
leaves into the microwave for very short bursts, thirty
seconds at a time, then taking it out and squeezing as
much liquid as you could from the parcel. Eventually
all the liquid and presumably most of the nutrients
were gone from the leaf and the dried remnants could,
so he was told, be chopped up into a powder. The
pop star's brother had said to him, honestly mate, a
little bump of that stuff, the pure stuff, and it's like
– BANG, WHO TURNED THE DARK OUT? The story
always went down well, no matter that we'd heard it
all before. V was an amusing storyteller and despite
his tics, despite his occasionally rather anti-social
aspect, a hugely likeable man. Was it simply the oddly
made, slightly wrong-headed phrase that made people
laugh, I thought to myself now, or was it something
else? Could it be the sense of serious criminal
transgression, of boundaries being overrun that had
become embedded in the words and their own violation
of logic and syntax. Wasn't it all the same thing,
finally – the families littering beauty spots across the
country, Edward Abbey going out at night, pulling
up the wooden stakes developers had driven into the
ground to mark out a new road in the Arches National

Monument, pop stars on cocaine binges in Colombia, little bags of dog shit in the trees, V's parties in an ancient woodland, his lackadaisical leaving of bottles of opiates on the bar in full view of whoever cared to look, government officials breaking their own guidance during a global pandemic – that rules were not, in the end, intractable or unbending. Not for some, anyway. Perhaps they thought of it as daring. Something to do with the will, that what they desire comes inevitably to pass. But it was not the will, or talent, or courage. It was being born in possession. And not simply in possession of wealth, or material belongings, but of power and status, and an intimate knowledge of the rules and how the rules are made and how they are turned, at times, into a kind of game, a game in which there is, of course, another set of rules, the possession of which inevitably led to yet more accrual of power and more certainty that whatever came to pass you would be safe. That the stakes were not ever quite the same for everybody. They were taught to offer the defence of a sense of 'reason' which everybody was assumed to understand – saturated in the feeling of rightness that accumulated along with their selfhood. Their category, their taxonomy, in the ecosystem of capital, which called upon words like 'justice' and 'fairness' and 'order', but which ultimately knew these words were empty of meaning, was that of the who-says-so. They moved through the world in the knowledge that *it* worked for *them*. In the world of the owl and the rabbit the owl had it just as hard,

despite the shock and awe of the rabbit's demise –
long evenings quartering the fields, chicks with an
apparently endless hunger, the risk inherent in every
hunt. Both earned their merit. But for those born
happy, born lucky, born in the light – in the village the
saying used to be 'born on the right side of the Tring
road' – born of the wide streets with the big houses,
the rabbit, when called upon, came quietly.

PART TWO

Disturbed Earth

A week passed when I could barely leave the house.
I simply could not rouse myself sufficiently. I had felt
a kind of regression take place – the days had the
echo of a summer many years ago when I had found
myself in a similar situation. Living at my parents,
in a place that seemed emptied, my friends all gone,
other ways I might have been living playing out in
my imagination, while the hard, true facts of my tiny
life shrank around me. I was listless then, and found
myself the same now. I drank myself loose from the
arbitrary conceits of time – mealtimes, bedtimes,
the time of day. Nothing mattered aside sunrise and
sunset. I stopped reading, I emptied my mind. For
years I had felt a strange separation from the memory
of that previous period in my life. I looked on that
person as a stranger wearing vaguely similar clothes,
liking similar records and books. Now I felt the
memory pressing itself upon me. It felt suddenly and

profoundly true. But perhaps I had always been more closely aligned to that enervated version of myself than I cared to admit. Had I not, after all, consistently failed, consistently shirked and made excuses, consistently avoided making a break for it – whatever that might have involved. Perhaps the brief periods of energy, of reading, of writing, of thinking, perhaps they were the outlying facts of my nature, little spells of mania, or some illness of the spirit which excited the nerves into action. I thought to myself how strange it was that we had these reverberations of our different selves that sounded out across the different times of our lives. Here I was, shorn of responsibility, of use, of company, perhaps of purpose, and I suddenly felt acutely bound to the person I had been at that other, quite specific age.

By now, the three of us in the house were hardly talking and had fallen into a silent observation of each other's odd rhythms. It was as if each of us knew the others' movements and with fastidious care avoided interrupting the rituals which had slowly replaced social interaction. After a week or more had passed without anything at all appearing to change – what I ate, how and when I slept, where I sat out the hours in the barren barroom – I snapped myself out of my lethargy. I decided to walk, a little drunk after an afternoon bout of boredom and tequila and tonics, up to the top of the hill and watch the sun go down behind the escarpment to the west. The horizon swallowed the last light in a flourish of gold and red and it was as if the neighbouring county was burning up. I felt quite suddenly the opposite of the overbearing solitude that had recently affected me sitting up there on the war memorial and looking out across the vale. All manner of life was around me up on the hilltop and down in the valley below. All infinite possibility. The dumb and the drunk. The deluded and the dead.

* * * *

There were two fields, one to the north, one to the south, intersected by the road that ran through the middle of the village, a road that was both a high street, and so the locus of all commerce, the façade of our place, and also, on the maps, a section of the Ridgeway – the ancient track that had itself once signified trade, goods, wealth, the movement of things. I took the path off the road just after the bridge across the bypass and headed towards the field to the south. A month or so ago, you could have walked right across the field, the footpath marked with an old sign at one edge, and then declaring itself in bright white chalk through the lush early summer grass liberally yellowed with buttercups. Now the whole field had been fenced off, the thick new wooden fence leading you right round its western edge and out through a metal gate on the southern side. Half of the field had been excavated and churned into huge dry clods. The earth was grey and dusty as concrete. The very way that I could take, the way that was being permitted, was in the process of being managed. Even out of doors, away, so we were told to think, from the petty boundaries of settlement – the gardens with their hedges, the car-parking spaces, the delineation of 'ours' and 'yours' – even here in what passed rather pathetically for the wild, I was affronted by enclosures, restrictions, reminders that all land was property, a fact of administration, the topographic expression of our cultural history and continued addiction to possession and allocation. Mary Austin wrote of the Californian desert, though she took issue with that name, 'Not the law but the land sets the limit.' Here the very opposite was true. The land hereabouts was as much a legal document as a geographical phenomenon, though it was also true that the fields were a kind of desert, evidenced by the absence now of so many of the birds and butterflies and insects that had once proliferated here.

These two fields I mention had become, over the previous few weeks, sites of some interest to me. I had watched as temporary offices were erected along with the fences. Portakabins and Portaloos, markers, engines, diggers, tools, power cables. All the trappings of what had we had for so long come to believe was development. Cars and pickup trucks, men in hi-vis and hard hats. They stood, they talked. They indulged in the strange rituals that made up what was called work, but that in fact were forms of socialising, of

establishing or retaining contact. I was reminded
once more, watching these work parties and their
preparations of the slipperiness of that word 'work', of
its usefulness to those in possession of wealth, to those
whose interests lie in what felt like an increasingly
anachronistic balance of infinite growth and the
destruction of things. This specific work was all part
of the building of the new railway. It was an irony not
lost on anyone round here that the government's two
biggest projects (or what were their biggest projects
until a virus arrived to undermine so much that they
had come to think and to prioritise) seemed to face in
opposite directions. How strange it was, to find myself
deep in the Brexit badlands, facing up to a debased
future for the hills and woods that I had loved all my
life thanks to an engineering project designed to tie
us to the same continent and cultures which so many
who lived here had spent the previous years, the years
since the referendum, denigrating. The demands of
globalism co-opted the parochial even as they laughed
in its face. These weren't the turkeys that voted for
Christmas exactly, but instead those who, voting
against it, found Christmas tunnelling its way into
the roost nevertheless. For these past few years HS2
had loomed overly large in the village, first merely as
an idea, as argument, as petition, but gradually it had
taken on a physical reality. Multicoloured scarves were
tied to trees in the woods in protest, large banners
along the London road denounced the destruction of
habitats and the devaluing of homes. In a small copse

between this village and the next a camp of protestors had established itself over one winter. Along the road that ran up to the hill a row of cottages sat empty after being compulsorily purchased. Round the corner from these, houses close to the route that didn't quite qualify for the government's purchasing scheme had For Sale signs displayed in their front gardens for a year or more, slowly to be replaced with ones that read To Let as buyers could not be found. Only a matter of months ago people in the Lantern talked about it as if it were the only cloud on the horizon. Any old man would be happy to tell you the difference between a slurry tunnel boring machine and an Earth Pressure Balanced tunnel boring machine – £25,000 or £22,000 per route metre of tunnel dug respectively, and that without taking into account the fixed costs of the machines themselves, the site maintenance, the disposal of excavated material and the cost of dropping in the high-voltage power lines the machines would require to do their work. For some all this meant an act of vandalism that amounted to the end of the place as they knew it. Or as they imagined it. I thought of Monkey Wrench Mark, who I saw often, out walking at the same times as me, taking food or other useful stuff out to the camp of protestors on the Missenden road. The last time it had been a set of curtains he'd had in his backpack, promised to one of the protestors for the treehouse they had built. They don't want alcohol, though, he told me. He described them as serious, professional. Some were veterans of numerous camps protesting environmental or cultural damage across the country for years. Others had followed the route of the HS2 work as it made its way up across the South Downs, pitching up wherever they could make their presence felt, wherever the project was set to scar the landscape. For others in the village the whole thing was a purely financial conundrum. They had a house they couldn't sell. They thought property prices would plummet as the village became blighted by the noise of fourteen trains an hour coming through at 250 mph. All through lockdown the work on HS2 had continued along the whole route – work that was deemed, as it must have been then, 'essential'. The essential work of a culture that still lusted after the earth through increasingly desperate, palmed-off, colonial gestures – exploitation, domination, commerce, cost-value, extraction, efficiency, profit. Gestures that seemed to be emptying themselves of potency day by day and yet still carried on. People despaired but did nothing. What could they do? What could any of us do? I stood and watched those men in the fields, thought of the machines that would soon be moving through the layers of rock below us, of all the money it involved, and it seemed hallucinatory, as if part of a dream of the world as I recalled it before those past few months of the virus and its suspension of things. It had been a world in which constant expansion was so often the apparently inarguable fact, the unassailable position – progress must not be hampered, civilisation must spread. Though it felt like a whole country, or more

accurately a whole workforce, was being held in a kind
of stasis, in a suspension of time, there was also the
looming possibility that maybe, after all this, there
wouldn't be any work to get back to. But perhaps it
was the case that people had long since grown sick of
doing their work. Maybe that sense of confusion, of
uncertainty, of an inarticulable loss was somehow to
be perceived in the protests that had filled the news
in those weeks – alongside the constant coverage of
the virus – in the anger, the palpable feeling that
profound and lasting and necessary changes of all
sorts were imminent and necessary. At the same time,
I read in the papers every day that we had among the
worst death rates in the world, that our economy was
to suffer more than any other country in Europe and
I wondered to myself what sense a word like 'profit',
or 'progress', would make after all this. How would
these things, so central for so long, be discerned or
fully understood, when their old metrics and internal
logic might all have been shown up as meaningless,
as props for systems suddenly obsolete and fragile.
But all words had become strange, that much was also
true, and I found myself at times staring at the pages
of books or magazines and finding the black marks on
the paper resistant to comprehension, turned somehow
obscure, illegible.

The field to the north of the road lay down a little
dirt track, more chalk, more flints, and just past the
main cricket ground. It was a kind of mirror image

of the southern field. The same trucks, the same
ephemeral erections, the sketch-work of buildings.
The footpath here, that ran around the base of the hill,
through Coneycroft farm, had now been cordoned off
by thick fencing. Larks here in the late afternoons,
and on a couple of evenings when I stopped at the
cricket club and waited and watched, I would see a
barn owl cruising over the long grass in the field. I
sat on the concrete steps of the pavilion and looked
down the slight incline on the outfield, across the
pitch, beyond the boundary to the north. I had spent
many, many hours here, both as child and adult. I
thought now of times when I watched the barn owls
here as a teenager, when I should perhaps have
been paying more attention to the game. Midweek
matches, when a young player might have been given
a chance in the first team, the game pushing its luck
with the light, and me fielding somewhere close to
the boundary, out of the action. And I remember
how on Saturdays, playing now in the full sun of the
afternoon, I would see mistle thrushes digging for
worms around the nets. I never saw them anymore,
but I recall my feelings about them then, recall
their size, their posture, their pale duns and their
freckled chest against the green grass. It will come
as no surprise, no doubt, to hear that a cricket club
in a place like this had its own ecosystem of various
statuses and snobberies. As children we were aware
of these gradations, that there were those of us from
the grammar school, and from the local comp, and that

there were those from even higher up the food chain – the public-school boys, who came to the game with a facility that was both enviable and unnerving. They had an ease with coaches and technique that I could never replicate. Perhaps that was where the difference lay – in an impression of the game as coming easy. We knew where we all stood within this framework, how our behaviour would be policed by various degrees according to our place, how our voices and accents and names had their sinister, perpetual, inevitable impacts. There were a handful of players, for instance, who might find they never quite fit in – a pair of brothers who lived a few doors down from my grandfather on the council estate, who could play but lacked kit, a couple of Asian kids from one of the larger local towns who found the club's parental cliques impossible to fathom. And me, who, being brought up in the pub, came from a kind of non-home, from a strange, uncategorisable place that resisted the other boys' – or their parents' – rigid sense of our childhood social position. I felt these things sharply when I was young. That my parents' work prevented them from attending games, that they didn't belong to the tennis club, that the other parents moved in different circles. I was sharply aware of things like my mother's tattoos. My father's long hair. But the feeling dissipated as I grew, and the adult cricket team, which had felt so intimidating at one time, turned out to be a kind of haven for misfits as well as for the grammar-school kids back from the universities in summer. I played for a few years, for instance, with a man called Robert, though everyone called him Bob. Bob Glue. I still saw him now and then in the Lantern. He was older than me and many of the other players in that team and I remember the first day he came to the club. He had his youngest daughter in a pram and stowed away on the shelf beneath the baby's seat a slab of cans of lager. He stood for a Saturday afternoon and drank his beer and watched the game. He joined the club soon after and I spent every Saturday and most Sundays with him for the next few years. He had, he told us, been a very good player in the years before we met, in his salad days, and his four front teeth were missing from when he had let one burst through his gloves while keeping wicket to his brother as a young man. He'd gone off, he used to tell us, had thirty stitches in his mouth, and come back to the game to bat. Played again Sunday. That night he couldn't get drunk, he said, so for the first time in his life he'd tried tequila. A bottle of it and he didn't feel a thing. He'd tried false teeth for a while but he lost them or they lost him. Bob was a house husband, looking after his six kids while his wife ran a burger van out on the way to Oxford.

Late afternoon and evenings, with the pubs and restaurants now closed, with nowhere to go but the air full of warmth and lengthening light, I sometimes saw people, some of whom I knew, sitting on the pavilion steps. It was the re-enactment of a version of their teenage years. Cans in the park, long listless summer nights. No school, no work, no time. The pavilion's aspect was a little like that of the pub. The windows and scoreboard pannelled up, the square overgrown, the social function of the building redundant. It threw its shadow rather bitterly over the outfield. If nobody was there I stood in my old position at fine leg or paced out my old run-up and waited at the top of my mark as I had done countless times before. I thought about how it felt to be here just a decade or so ago, the same time of year, part of a long-disbanded team. So much was so different, and I remembered that what I felt keenest, most strongly, in those years when I had remained here in the village long after my friends and peers had left was a kind of profound safety. I could look up at the hills from the beer garden at the Lantern in the evenings, or from the cricket pitch, or walking along the towpath and perceive with a strange and deep intensity that nothing, somehow, could harm me here. I remembered talking to a friend who was working in central London at a bookshop on the day of the 7th July bombings in 2005. She told me how the shop had stayed open but they'd had no customers, how she'd felt sick all day with a nervousness she'd never known before. How she would forget about the morning's chaos for a minute, then remember it again with a sudden recall of pain and care and disbelief, and how that had gone on all day and for weeks afterwards. She told me how at the end of the day there had still been no public transport in the central part of the city, so she'd walked down towards the river where she could get a bus south and home from Waterloo station. She'd described how she'd crossed the bridge with thousands of other people, all walking the same direction, the visible emptying of a whole city. And I remembered at that time being relieved that I lived here in this small, inconsequential place. A place defined even now, with the world sick and burning itself up with the anger of those who have been robbed of ever knowing that very same sense, by its fundamentally being safe. Poverty, war, famine, even a global pandemic. Nothing would ever fully penetrate us here. Perhaps that's why people were so affronted by the train line coming, by the desecration of the hills and fields. Not because they loved these things, but because they believed, somewhere deep within themselves, that they should be beyond the reach of politics. The hammer should continue to fall elsewhere, as it always had. Standing on the outfield I realised though that there were things I missed deeply even among all this that I had come to despise. There was nothing simple, I understood then, in the connections I had to this place, which must be the same for everyone who lived there, perhaps for anyone who lived anywhere. Inarticulate and angry, heartsore and defeated. Caught between history and the swiftness with which the summers of our own life pass. I felt suddenly very old.

* * * *

Mid-June and the weather gave in. Finally, rain. Storms began to appear in the afternoons as if from nowhere, rolling in over the hills, dragging their dark nimbus over the plantation conifers and squatting over the village for a few hours until the evenings. The parties on the cricket pitch dissipated, BBQ fuel lasted longer than an hour or two on the local shops' shelves. The weather had forced us back into the forlorn and dusty saloon of the pub. The days grew Scrabble games and air-pressure headaches. Afternoon naps. My mother's regime had by now become quite brutal. Walking early, she took a route she had devised that meant she had by the end of it climbed the equivalent of one hundred flights of stairs. Maybe storeys. I forget now the phraseology of the app that she used. She then did weights in the garden, and every other day a yoga class delivered over the internet to her laptop in the sports bar. This was, I am bound to say, the closest the room had come to living up to its name in a good while. Perhaps in fact since a dangerous, though enjoyable, amalgam of darts and bare knuckle boxing broke out between a couple of tree surgeons one afternoon a few years ago. At the time I was sitting at the bar and the boss of one of the local firms had brought his lads in to give them their Christmas drink. After taking a humiliating and interminable beating at darts by a particularly dislikeable youngster, the boss in question decided that what my grandfather referred to as a round of knuckle sandwiches was required to even the scores.

They were asked to leave after the fracas broke out in the bar, but I heard a week or so later from the one young man in the party who used the pub regularly, that his gaffer had fared just as badly in the fist fight which ensued once they had left the pub and found themselves out in the street. The all-round sporting excellence of his younger colleague made for a rather pinched Christmas for all of them, as the boss took off to lick his wounds without doling out their drink.

My mother was flourishing while my father continued to brood. Dates for reopening were mooted, moved, ignored in the daily briefings. Anticipation, anxiety. Who would come anyway? Would we remember how we once were, how to be together? Would it be so bad if we'd forgotten? What would really be lost in the commonwealth of saloon bars like ours across the country if they were never to return? Once again I felt at odds with myself about the place. Sometimes these little rooms seemed defined by a kind of back-slapping homogeneity, an almost sinister sense of false security in walking into a room full of people who looked alike, who spoke the same language in the same accent, who read the same newspapers. The band of 'Petes' who would greet you upon entry, their pints of beer lined up on the bar, their navy blues, their racing greens, their checks and their browns, their irony, their comfort. It was as if, at times, the individual lives had begun to melt away into an illusion of half-felt affinity. But this could be a failure of my own memory as much as anything else. An inability, now, to pick out what was real and what was simple representation.

From the low path that skirted Coombe Hill you could see down the final few feet of the incline into the back gardens of the large, outermost houses of the village. One or two of the gardens had paths of their own that picked their way up onto the footpath, so that you could, should you fancy, walk out of the back door of your house in the morning, down the garden, which might in itself take ten minutes or more, through a small metal gate, or past a compost bin or two, and up into the hills. Some of those houses, if you will allow me to indulge a little snobbishness of my own, were somewhat displeasing to the eye. Huge, square, redbrick monstrosities. They appeared ridiculous set against the hills. But one or two at least affected to acknowledge and even to defer to the vernacular building traditions of the area. Flint and brick walls. Thatch on the roofs. Here is where we housed our illustrious village residents. There were one or two well-known actors, a long-retired racing driver, a pop star whose fame had now dimmed, once renowned for his dancing, ostentatious headgear and predilection for sports cars. He, in particular, would regularly be seen driving around the area in one or other of his extensive collection. I recall an occasion when I was young and on a night out in the local town, when a few of us were in the queue to get into the one nightclub. It was a rather run-down place at that time, but not without its pretensions. A shabby red carpet lined the street outside where we were to queue. The sign had its neon and diamanté. The name itself a dash of French, an accent somewhere. These kinds of places always seemed to me to communicate in the most direct and immediate way the truly parochial nature of towns like ours. The music was awful, the clientele a narrow section of the populace, and at that time they seemed obsessed with an arbitrary set of rules about dress. No trainers, for instance. Shirts with a collar. No jeans. The occasion I was recalling then was a year or so after we had all left school. The bouncers were arguing the toss with the pop star and refusing him entry on account of his Adidas trainers. We all knew the ridiculousness of the situation. Inside, they would play one or other of his songs over the course of almost any night. In the same week, he would have been to any one of London's best clubs or restaurants or bars. But out here none of that mattered. The rule was everything for the doormen of the market towns of England, and the rule was – no trainers.

The front gardens of these houses were full of foxgloves and lupins, red valerian, big, old-fashioned roses. The back gardens were immaculately lawned, and from the path you could see the edge of a swimming pool here, the nut-coloured wood of an outdoor sauna building there. One of these houses I had once known well. It belonged, for the years of my childhood and on into adolescence, to the family of my friend Stephen. I had

met Stephen on my first day at the small school here
in the village and I still remember the occasion of him
asking me to come round to what he called 'the house'
for tea. In fact he used the phrase 'come up to the
house', and always did. And even then I understood
him to mean that the house was separate in some way
from other houses. It was elevated, lofty. We moved
here when I was about ten, leaving north London
where we'd lived in a council flat. For my mother it
had been a moving-back, a return to the place of her
birth, to where she still had a parent, and old friends,
an extended family that all lived in houses close to each
other up on the estate. For my father, I suppose, it had
simply been an opportunity. A pub that had always
done good business, a chance for a different kind of life
away from the city of his birth. Stephen had been a
strange boy when I first met him, somewhat outside of
the already firmly established social strata of the boys
and girls at the school. Like my own, his parents were
not the clubbable types. No tennis, no golf. I remember
how I thought from the first that he had unusual
interests – science, especially the natural world,
classical music – and he was physically awkward,
rather on the large side, unattractive, clumsy. He wore
a head brace at night to fix his riot of teeth. However,
he grew into one of the truly gilded youths of the local
grammar school, excelled as a scholar, especially in
the sciences, but in truth he could have picked any
academic path. He played rugby, and trumpet in the
school jazz band. It was Stephen who first aroused my

own interest in birds, when I suppose we were around twelve and we would watch them on the feeders in his garden and he would show off his knowledge of a few species and their songs. A strange competitiveness compelled me to try and amass a knowledge of my own that might rival his, and I would sit and read the bird and animal and plant books that filled one shelf of the many in his house. The garden would be visited by an array of birds I had never seen in The Paper Lantern's beer garden, and it was there I saw many firsts – sparrowhawk, nuthatch, little owl, treecreeper. I recall the day we saw the first of the kites that had now become commonplace, and our exhilaration at the sight. Oddly, however, it was not Stephen but his mother who came most often into my thoughts. She was a brilliant woman, somewhat flamboyant, who had interests of her own that seemed to fill the house. She made sculptures from scrap metal – always animals such as horses or deer or antelope, she painted watercolours of the garden for which she had a profound love, and she was an excellent cook. I remember the bright yellows and greens of her clothes, her thin hair, which she kept short. She would tell us of her own childhood in Kenya, how she had learned about the birds and animals she had grown up surrounded by and how she felt that it was somehow proper we feel the same way about our own species. She would laugh at our excitement at the little brown jobs of the English woodland, but at the same time she would say that these things, these plants, these birds, were the stuff from which each of you is built. She said that looking properly, looking with attention, with care, at the world was a way of absorbing it into yourself, taking on its largesse, its fullness. She would say that every time you notice a wild flower, the exact colour it offers up say, or its scent, or the way it attracts a certain specific set of insects, the way it grows in the shadow of a certain tree, this is how you fill yourself with the world. Consider what most people spend their lives looking at, she said. Meaningless things. When people travel they use it as an excuse to buy a new camera. People spend their lives devoted to pets, and don't see the tiny insects all around them. She said that at the end, what you are is the accumulation of these things – these occasions of note, each sight or smell or sensation that excites your touch. It's not to do with knowing them as names, she would say, it's about individual experiences. She told me once, finding me with yet another of her books in my hand, that I read too much. Living and thinking are at odds, she said to me with a laugh, put the bloody books away and go outside.

Stephen's father was an executive for an oil company, and his parents had met while his father was working for a while in Mombasa. They had photos of their wedding up on a side table in their dining room. I remember best the one with Stephen's father in some sort of traditional Kenyan dress, a loose shirt of an earthy, orange colour, with Stephen's mother and her sisters stood around him. There was an unmistakable, exuberant happiness to the photograph, and the infinitely hopeful moment it had captured. But there was something about it, too, that always left me feeling melancholic. It seemed to singularly communicate to me the distance that these people had travelled, the way they had moved across the earth, the things they'd had to leave behind at each stop, pressured by their own individual needs and the forces that propelled and jostled them along as part of a vast, interconnected financial machine. And by other, more prosaic things, of course – circumstance, family, love. There was something of the spent summer in that photograph, and indeed in many of the things around the house that made me think of, or imagine, their old life in Kenya, a life of which Stephen had no recollection, no knowledge. What I found myself bringing back to mind most often about his mother, however, was the time in my final year of school when I had got into the habit of skipping my art lessons. I'd fallen out with my teacher over a project and had disappointed him by declaring my intention not to go to art school, and in fact expressing my doubts about the nature of university at all. On those days I would leave school at lunchtime and walk alone down to the bus stop and wait for the bus home. Every now and then, Stephen's mother would drive past and she would always stop and offer me a lift. She would have been into the town to get her shopping and I would help her unload it at the house and walk back down into the village. Driving back that particular day, as I remember it now, she asked me why I didn't yet drive myself and I told her that I'd tried taking my test a couple of times and failed, after which it had become a source of anxiety and stress. I said I'd get my exams out of the way and perhaps think about it again over the summer. I didn't tell her that I had no interest in driving, that I had already, even at that young age, come to think that I would be quite happy if I never had to travel further from the village than I could walk in a day. She said something to me then that surprised me, given that we were driving still close to a reasonably large town along a busy main road, past schools, shops, even a police station. She told me, quite directly, that she herself couldn't wait to get her licence, to pass her test so that she could drive further afield than the shops in town without feeling worried about the police or Stephen's father, or for that matter Stephen himself, finding out she'd taken her car out. I remember the laughter which accompanied the telling. And yet she seemed so casual, so nerveless. I promised her I wouldn't tell Stephen that I'd seen her out driving if, in turn, she didn't tell my own mother she'd seen me out of school.

Walking that same path in the mornings as I now did, compulsively, habitually, faithfully, I looked down the hill and once more into that garden in which I spent so much time in my childhood. What was it that felt alien about the place now, I wondered. Was it the passing of time that had somehow altered the nature of the place, or was it that its people had changed? The people I knew were long gone and I could not conceive of myself walking down the little goat path, as we used to call it, and into the garden, walking up to the back doors of the house and simply announcing my entrance. To have been able to do so even once felt as imaginary, as impossible, as if I were to do it now. And yet that's how it would have been. It was a further failure to no longer be able to summon up a true sensation, how things were, in this house quite unlike all the other homes that I had known. The always-open door, the freedom of its space, its seemingly innate sense of knowledge, its geography, its books and its birds.

Above me a buzzard held itself against the wind, fanned its tail like a kestrel, watched the earth below, reading it with an accuracy I could only guess at. I wondered at the effort it took the bird to still its head, to ride the updraughts from the face of the scarp with its wings, which unlike those of the falcon it seemed to be aping, were not uniquely designed for the task. The wings folded slightly as if the bird had become suddenly self-conscious at my thought, it banked in the air and before I could take five more steps it was out of sight around the bend of the hill.

There was more and more talk now of the possibility of travel in the news, in the little meetings outside shops and the cafés on the high street. Tentative suggestions of summer holidays and overseas visits as the lockdown

measures began to ease. Over these past few months
so much that seemed necessary once just seemed to
me futile and pathetic. Multiple family holidays to
ever more exotic destinations, sales trips to America,
China, Dubai. Second homes in the Caribbean. Cruises.
I'd heard them all talked about and pored over from
either side of the bar in the Lantern, but just as the
customers themselves had disappeared, I wondered
if all that excess, all that money and burned fuel and
waste and consumption were set to be no more than the
substance of memory. I had never really fixed myself
on anywhere to go, never committed myself, and so
travel became just another set of abstract ideas for me
to walk with in my imagaination. I wonder now if I
had always felt this way about it. Reluctant to leave.
When the world locked itself down, I felt curiously in
step. I thought about why it made me uneasy, the idea
of being elsewhere, of leaving home. I thought of my
parents' annual trips to America, the places and things
I believed at one time I might myself want to see, the
story of Stephen's parents meeting. How was it that
his dad had found himself in Kenya, was it enough
to simply say that oil had brought him there? Or was
there something more meaningful, more strange, in
that flow of resources, of goods and finance and people
which had been so central to them, to everything their
lives had come to be? I thought of my grandmother,
my mother's mother, who by her own peregrinations
made her way here to this inconsequential little village
in England from Macau, and found herself greeted, no

doubt, with suspicion, with gossip, dark-skinned and foreign-tongued as she was. And I thought about how life almost repeated itself in these odd ways, but with subtle alterations, with those shifts of light and time and space that meant the repetition was never true, never exact, that the note had changed in some small, but always noticeable way, throughout the musical phrase of history.

* * * *

Long hot days. Mornings in the woods and afternoons on the towpaths. Watering on the allotment. More dog shit in the bushes. Beer bottles and a Robinsons Fruit Shoot on the floor of a small clearing. Silence. More silence. Long, slow silence that ran into long, warm nights.

* * * *

If you were to mark its position on a map of the country, the village would be just about dead centre, depending, to a certain extent, on your definition of the centre. A tiny little hamlet just to the east along the ridge of hills was always held, around here at least, to be the furthest point from the sea on all sides in the whole country. Middle England, middle earth, middling, mediocrity. The Ordnance Survey disagrees, however, much to the annoyance of certain regulars in the pub who maintained the local claim. Odd, these little points of pride in our own peculiar places, the details which we cling to for comfort, to assure us we are not living out our days of nothingness in a nowhere to match. Every morning I took my first piss of the day in the saloon bar toilets and looked up at the wall to my right, which had been papered with a huge OS map of the area surrounding the village. The Three Hundreds of the Aylesbury Vale. Perhaps I have been a little unfair on my father with regards to his interests, for he had always had a love of maps. The pub, for instance, contained a small collection of OS maps of the area that served, variously, as a diversion for drinkers, a point of interest for visitors from elsewhere, and occasionally for the regulars to indulge their memories, to unfold and reorient themselves and their pasts, to show some one of us where they once lived, or where their parents had their first house, where the old school was, where the legendary pub just outside the village used to stand before it was permanently closed and the very nature of the building changed forever. The collection goes back as far as an old New Popular Edition One-Inch Map of the area from 1945. The area is the Chilterns, or the North Chilterns, or most latterly Chiltern Hills North – Explorer number 181. Some mornings I would take a map down and plot a route out over a long-gone version of the same ground I walked each day. On the old maps, the nature of the space seemed both improbable and familiar. Huge expanses of pale fields between this village and the next, and yet, for the most part, the demarcations were similar enough. Hedges ran the same lengths, field patterns remained unaltered. I looked at how the village had, by now though, leached out over the fields and had propagated itself alongside the canal and main roads, outgrown its original dwellings and the traces left behind. These changes were essays of their own, essays on commerce and human geography and military history. The hamlet that once neighboured the village along the hills to the east had, over the last fifty or so years, been swallowed by its RAF base and the slow expansion of our own borders. On one of the old maps it was simply the big Rothschild house, a couple of farms and a row of cottages on the canal. I thought how different the map would look again in a couple of years, with the new high-speed train line completed and a new set of marks on the page – access roads, tracks, a copse or two vanished, meadows repurposed. But certainly there would be changes we could not now anticipate. What unpredictable damage would the next few years bring – damage that would surely alter both the maps and the lives of the place. HS2, leaving the EU, the lingering effects of the disease and its overwinter implications.

I walked south-west, away from the field that had by now been almost entirely peeled back to what looked, in the exacting light of the longest day of the year, like the bones of the earth. The white of the chalk exposed, piles of grey soil along the meadow's edge.

Along the perimeter fence that had been erected over the previous fortnight, one or two tunnel entrances had already appeared under the wooden fencing. Most probably badgers, judging by the material deposited around the holes. A strange confluence then, in this field, of excavation, of the movement of soil, of the men above ground and the animals below, mirroring themselves in the bustle and energy of their work, the echoes of the other in the piles of earth, stone and detritus that marked their tasks. I thought of this long after I had left the field behind, when I was up into the woods that ran south away from the village, and as I passed the farms and rather remote houses of the next little hamlet. I took some strange comfort in the badgers' earth-work, in the fact of their own efforts to improve the land for their own sakes. Perhaps my morbid, anthropocentric fixation on our own activity pertaining solely to the desecration of the earth was a misstep, perhaps I had been wrong about things. It would not be the first time. Perhaps our apparently rapacious assault on every resource available to us was simply a kind of steroidal nest-building. The badgers and rabbits and foxes and birds all left their own marks, after all.

I continued south-west across the hills, along a line that repeated itself across the maps that I pored over each morning. The roads, the footpaths, the rivers, the tracks – everything tended in this direction in this little corner of the hills. So it was with the patterns

of our way-making, overlaying themselves, one on
top of the other, replicating an unseen history, or
some aspect of topography that eluded the inexpert,
quotidian gaze. Hampdenleaf Wood, Little Hampden
Common, Little Hampden Farm. Eventually I came
to a place overwritten on the map by its human
connections, Little Hampden and Great Hampden,
the villages to the north and south of Hampden House.
Exiting a copse and crossing a couple of fields planted
with field beans, it was the road up to the great
house that became visible first – that long, straight
driveway that so often attends the grand old English
country house, that carried, for so long and with such
conviction, the impression of dignity and bearing
which obfuscated, in so many cases, generations of
swindling, slavery, exploitation and jealously guarded
inheritance. The house here was the ancestral home
of the Hobart-Hampdens, a family who owned this
land even before the Norman conquest and who finally
vacated the house in 1938. By then they had been
earls and politicians, revolutionaries, exiles, plotters,
chancellors. The proximity of politics and crime, of
power and violence, of wealth and exploitation – it
was all there in the histories of the great and the
good, baked into the bricks of these places, trod into
the soil. Perhaps the best known of the family was
John Hampden, known colloquially as 'the Patriot',
for his refusal, and subsequent prosecution, to pay
ship money. He was an important figure in the
outbreak of the civil war, one of the Five Members

whose attempted arrest by King Charles precipitated the outbreak of war, and his death in battle was considered at the time to be a great loss. The primary school in the village, which we all attended before taking the exam which then separated us off into our various future lives, was named for him, so too the big pond by the church. Look again at the map and you found you were never too far from his name.

I walked alongside the drive, on the footpath up to the church that sat adjacent to the house. Strange and sad and beautiful, this old building in the bright sun. Thirteenth century. I found a bench in the graveyard where John Hampden was buried and thought of him dying in the Greyhound Inn in a town a little further to the west. And I thought of him as he appears on his statue in the centre of the town, sword in his right hand, his left hand pointing. Towards what? The enemy? The battlefield? Or a kind of imagined future, perhaps, a posited version of England without a despotic, unelected royalty, with a more robust democratic process. Someone in the pub told me once that the sculptor had him pointing to the Houses of Parliament. History, of course, does not always play to the tune of the hopes and dreams of revolutionaries, and here I sat on the same patch of England as his, still blighted by a bloated and outdated royalty, an aristocracy that have used the death and disease and austerity and child poverty of their own time as no more than markets with which to gamble and increase their wealth. More hierarchies to undermine the ecstatic potential of life. This land should have read that day of the beech trees in their luminous pomp, the unseen skylark's song, the hobby catching swifts midair. Instead it was a crudely written treatise on rank, on cap-doffing, on titles and tithes. I began to think of the other statues that decorated the town centre. They were of a very different order altogether. There was David Bowie, in a multitude of his best-known guises, on a rather hidden-away wall that led down to the cinema and the Wagamama and Gourmet Burger Kitchen – a memorial that has, for some peculiar reason, elicited numerous remonstrations in the form of graffiti daubed on the wall or on the floor at the singer's feet. Based on these constantly updated scribblings, one could only surmise that the people of the town had taken umbrage at Bowie for all manner of imagined wrongs – HS2, food banks, climate change – all ceremoniously laid at the feet of the artist. Or perhaps it was simply the fact of a statue's existence at all, any statue, a symbol of public expenditure, of frivolity and waste. The town's other notable bronze was one of the actor Ronnie Barker sitting on a bench by the new theatre, looking up at the building. These two odd icons told their own tale of the sort of absence of authentic selfhood that had come upon those middle-English market towns. The high streets all identical, depressed, slowly emptying. The young drained away to the cities. Neither Bowie or Barker were born there, neither lived there. The town had appropriated their image, in lieu of any more compelling recent history, based on the first performance of Bowie's Ziggy Stardust character at the old Civic Centre, and an early turn in the town by Ronnie Barker in his reparatory theatre days. To me, there was something poignant about these monuments to the town's lack. They seemed to announce, in their own way, that the town had indeed produced nothing of note save its own ease, its own comfort. No art, no culture, no politics, not even a sports team to speak of. Sometimes it felt as if, were you to look closer at the map, you would find, in fact, that there was nothing there at all. That perhaps the whole vale was a mistake, a smudge below the hill line, a false memory, a fantasy, a lie.

Hampden House was empty most of the time now and its only use was as a high-end wedding venue. Today it looked out of place somehow – it had an emptiness coaxial with its size. Its buttery-yellow paintwork looked garish in the sunlight. Like the pub, its whole function felt suddenly undermined by the events of recent history. Not just the disease though here, but perhaps the movements of the whole period since the Hampden family left. The financial problems that caused them to leave, the South Sea Bubble, the First World War, the Depression. The house stood there like an obsolete piece of machinery in the corner of a field. Its connections had become meaningless, its meaning now was as a symbol of one, increasingly degraded, version of the past. The kings and queens

and princes who visited, the oddities of the building –
a tower, for instance, built from 'clunch', a vernacular
Buckinghamshire building material made of chalk
and mud, the place might as well have been a dubious
and long-forgotten entry in a book, a figment of fable.
It was hard, even sitting there now and looking at the
place, to truly believe in it.

I recalled the wedding of a couple of regulars from
the Lantern that took place in the house a number
of years ago. The morning of the ceremony, a coach
had picked thirty guests up from the pub and my dad
had put on bacon sandwiches and opened the bar
for anyone who wanted an early start. The groom
was a high-ranking officer in the RAF, stationed
at the base in the neighbouring village. The bride
wasn't a local girl, but she was very well liked. As I
remember it now, the day had for me the qualities
of something from a previous period in history, as if
the whole population of the village had attended and
experienced a certain, very specific, simultaneous,
ritual exultation, something deeply felt, communal.
I had thought on the day that there could be no
stronger connection between those of us in attendance,
all of our own small and unimportant little places,
drinking and dancing in the rooms of that huge
and overpowering house. I thought for a moment
that I had come to understand something of the
function of these rituals, and these buildings, how
they transmitted their energy across whole groups

of people. But afterwards I had felt a strange kind of sadness whenever I recalled the day. All I could ever seem to bring to mind was the sense, in the weeks that followed, that what had seemed in all the individually experienced moments of the day itself to be a transformative, profound occurrence had dissolved somehow into a folk-memory made of sentiment, show and expense. People talked only of the cost of it all, the extravagance. The couple moved away and nobody heard much from them again. Gossip and rumour a couple of years later. The same old weaknesses of masculinity, ego, infidelity and waste. Photographs, in the end, of his dick on another woman's phone.

* * * *

A dawn chorus of pure wood pigeon. From somewhere far off, as if in an instantly forgotten dream I heard five, six, perhaps as many as a dozen birds close to the window, calling. When I did wake, I found the birds were still there, still sounding themselves. Some psychic link from the dream world to the here and now of the bright morning. The finches, the thrushes, the warblers had already given up the ghost for the summer. Perhaps for longer if the declining numbers of so many of them were to be believed. The pigeons, though, had grown fat and plentiful over the previous fifty or so years. Culvers, they were called by the old men on the allotments – occasionally other names beginning with 'c' if they

had taken particular liberties with the brassicas.
They had thrived since the agricultural revolution,
and gone on thriving as the fields had expanded, as
the nature of crops had changed, as their natural
predators had been killed off, as the gardens of
villages like this one had put out more and more
birdseed. I found these birds strange, and always
had – their cold stare ran right through me somehow.
I remember Stephen telling me, when we were quite
young, that doves and pigeons produce a kind of
milk, to aid them in the feeding of their chicks.
I can remember even at the time understanding that
fact as a challenge to how I'd imagined the things
of the world, and the uncanny sense it lent the
birds from then on in my imagination. When I was
older, deep in a spell of reading the likes of George
Lakoff and struggling my way through writing of
my own – undergraduate reading, really, alongside
pretentious and overwrought work, an attempt on
my part to keep up, somehow, with Stephen and the
others who had gone off to universities and cities and
real lives – I had hoped I might eventually clarify
for myself the complications I half perceived in how
words and names had been made, however ill-fitting,
to turn the living world into a grid of description, of
reference, of knowledge that had always rang, if not
false, then not quite true either. At the time, and
in fact it is probably still true now, I felt my way
into my own thoughts like somebody entering an
unfamiliar room in the dark, a little reticent, almost

fearful, palming my way round for objects to orientate myself. For my thoughts had always seemed to me half-formed, or perhaps more accurately, half-lit, and I was afraid of their shortcomings. It seemed to mean something to me that here was a bird that produced milk, like a mammal would, something I could almost comprehend, and which, if I could indeed grasp, would resolve a particular anxiety I had always carried around with me. A frustration, a knot in the stomach that seemed to centre around the insufficiency of words to capture the nature of things. I thought hard and habitually about those animals that pushed at the edges of their categorisation. Birds that did not fly, fish that could breathe out of water. It seemed of a piece to me with that photograph I had seen of the Rothschilds having their trap pulled by zebras – these animals that were almost horses, but not quite, doing the horse's work. And wasn't there something about that flourish of nonconformity that carried the same sense that I was stretching for? Something in every eccentric detail, in every distinct thing. The implication in all this, to me, was of life's true state as that of abandon, of infinite wildness, of always fighting its way out of the smothering, shrinking, tendency of taxonomy. Of a fundamental way of knowing the earth, and the life of it, that was different to simply naming and organising. Stephen and I had long conversations on the matter when we were teenagers. A favourite topic of Stephen's, for instance, was the question of when a certain

stage of an animal or plant's evolution progressed
from one category of taxonomy into another, newer
one. I wondered about that word 'progressed', and
how it conjured with our ideas of time as well as
space, how we so easily believed that the changing
nature of a physical object as time passed could
always be made to fit into the word. Again, it seemed
to fall short. My thinking on all this, as had so
commonly been my failing, abandoned me – perhaps
my grasp of things was what had in fact fallen short.
In turn I eventually gave up on that work and reading
like so much else, and came to despise everything
I'd written around the period. Stephen went on to
study seriously those things that had once been the
topics of our first forays into seemingly immense
and purposeful conversations, at Oxford as a zoology
student, then at Imperial College, London, where
his first postgraduate degree was in taxonomy,
biodiversity and evolution. When we did still see each
other, in those days, around the time he was finishing
his doctoral thesis, we would carry on our talk about
the philosophical and scientific implications of these
categories – conversations from our adolescence that
his work enabled him, then, to see both the usefulness
and the limitations of. His thinking seemed clear
in some way I could not emulate. In those long, late
conversations deep into the night, at a table in the
Lantern after closing time when he was back home to
visit, he made me feel as if I would never attain the
same clarity of thought as he seemed so effortlessly

capable of. I relished those times and loved to be in the company of his brain.

Perhaps it was too simple to conflate these ideas of order and empire, of biological or geographical neatness as simply another expression of whatever flaw it was that compelled those particular people to attempt to describe and contain, and ultimately perhaps to claim as their own, the places and things of the world. Categories, borders, rules, even mealtimes all came with a hidden function. I thought for example, was there anything so depressing as the notion of a passport? There'd been an argument about them one evening in the pub. Of course it had to do with the European question, and most of the men in the bar were adamant that they wanted their old-fashioned blue passports back. I was silent, but in the privacy of my thoughts I couldn't help but think the whole bunch of them had succumbed to a kind of madness. Was that what they really thought of when they imagined themselves as human beings in the world? A little book whose pages pastiched money and whose covers pastiched leather and which declaimed all the smallness of their lives and their history in a set of stamps. They were welcome to it. Despite having voted the same way as the others, though for very different reasons, that night Monkey Wrench Mark, as was frequently the case, found himself in on the argument. He had never had a passport, he said. He'd not needed one when he came here with

his parents as a child, and he'd refused at all times
to have one. He went on to argue that a passport was
documentary proof that you had succumbed to and in
fact approved of everything that had destroyed our
understanding of the true nature of the world. Private
property, nationhood, barriers, enclosure. He told
us that night, and I had heard him talk about this
before, that one of his favourite things to do when he
was out on his walks was to try and find ways onto
private land – the big houses, the National Trust
properties, country clubs, private woods, that sort
of thing. He would find a way in and simply walk
around. He said that when he did that, he felt every
step of the ground beneath his feet in a new, modified
way. He was suddenly aware of himself – at times
scared, and at times jubilant. It sounded to me very
much how I had often thought it would feel to be
overseas. One of the sites that he regularly used to
trespass on was called West Wycombe Park, a good
number of miles away to the east of the village across
the hills. He had found a way over the walls and into
the gardens, and would wait until after the National
Trust's visiting hours were over and make his way
onto the grounds. He'd walk the park alone and sleep
out in just a bivvy bag he took with him everywhere
he went. Every footstep on those grounds, he told us
once, was his small rejection of the idea of ownership
of that land, or any land. He took a particular delight
in his trespassing there, he said, because the house
and grounds had once been owned by the Dashwood

family, one of whom, Sir Francis Dashwood, the second baronet, had been, during his lifetime, a noted libertine, founding a club which much later became known as the Hellfire Club. Monkey Wrench Mark loved the idea of performing his own freedom to walk and think and sleep where he chose in the very same location in which this aristocrat had once lived out his own fantasies of Rabelaisian liberty and transgression. Drink, prostitutes and banquets as well as rumours of black masses and magical practice were all part of the club's activities, which, after several venues, eventually held its meetings in a series of tunnels and caves in the hills around the house and nearby village. These had been dug out of the hills in the eighteenth century to provide chalk for road-building and to provide work for the local people, who had suffered several years of drought and disastrous crops. The same Dashwood family had once also owned the big house to the north-east of the village, whose grounds ran down to the canal side, and I often thought of these competing histories when I walked along that stretch of water, or up the little wood that ran off the towpath into the hills, with its adventitious crop of yew trees at the entrance. These histories, I thought, were never simply actions from a separate past, but strands of incident and intention that lay across time, which even now play themselves out. The ownership of property, of land, of goods, of money, of people. None of this was ever truly relegated simply to the past, no more than it was possible to ever truly 'get over it', as you might hear your argument or thought dismissed with in the Lantern. There was in fact, no such thing as the past when it came to the disaster of empire and capital – just a long and terminal present.

* * * *

I left the pub one day and headed north. I came to the end of South Street and turned right onto the main road running down the hill and through the village. Mid-morning and the streets were busy once again. The two or three coffee shops had been allowed to open and had people sat outside, the Post Office reopened, one or two small shops had started to trade again. We had, in what struck me then as quite a short time really, evolved a kind of outdoor version of all our indoor methods and modes of living. People met in the parks and beauty spots, they sat on the benches outside the shops, or down by the clock tower. There was a rumour that the area outside the small supermarket and pharmacy, a sort of market square called Manor Waste, would soon be turned into an outdoor dining area for the three restaurants and the deli nearby. There was an excitement behind the rumour, a sense of novelty, of a kind of imported Europhile glamour. Another little irony to enjoy – that in this emblematic middle-English village, this land of Leave-and-the-French-second-home-be-damned, the people still yearned for what amounted

to a greyer, colder version of Europe. I remembered
an argument in the Lantern once between a couple
of the younger regulars and a much older man called
Ron. Ron had been an accountant in his youth, and
by his own reckoning – plausible too – cut quite a
dash in his day. He had his stories about growing up
around Fulham and Shepherd's Bush, and especially
about his glory days under Thatcher when he made
his money and spent his time in London casinos and
drove sports cars, an exhaustive list of which he would
be only too happy to provide. His one truly great story
was of dancing with the actress Ava Gardner on an
aeroplane. These days he would come into the pub
very late every night and have his couple of pints, no
more, before driving up the hill back to his cottage.
That particular evening he came in, found only Tom
and Jim at the bar, and the three of them spent an
hour or so talking about how Ron had voted to leave
the EU in the referendum, and about his subsequent,
and immediate, application for an Irish passport via
some spurious relative, along with the same for his
kids, in order that they could still travel as extensively
as they were accustomed to. The two sides of the
debate were drawn as crudely as that – the young
against the old, just as a lamentable news media
would have us believe the split was playing out at the
time across the whole country. No real complexity,
no surprises. I listened to the arguments but did not
offer my thoughts. It is not quite true of me to say that
there was nothing surprising about the interaction

between the three of them however, because they subsequently became close friends. It would be quite common, on the recent long warm nights, to see Jim and Tom sitting out on the cricket pitch with a bag full of beers and at about nine o'clock to see a large car pull up and Ron unfold his rangy frame from the front seat, carrying a bottle of white wine of his own over to the boys. I thought about the three of them sitting and drinking together, talking about football, about Ron's days out watching Fulham and eating fish and chips at the Seashell by Marylebone station, about Jim's love of horse racing and about pubs and HS2, and it seemed to me that they had, in their own way, rejected the taxonomy of so much of our socialised selves. And even, almost unbeknown to them, they had rejected the taxonomies of their own prejudices. Youth and old age, class, geography. The peculiar and unconnected ways they had each come to be here, and to know each other's company, are facts of exactitude, not category – they had outgrown their original, almost archetypal, interaction at the bar and had begun to experience one another through an odder, more particular relationship. I could not help but find, when I thought of how we lived here, that I felt something like gratitude for these two young men and their much older friend. The fact of this friendship, strange as it might have seemed, deepened my own connection to this place somehow, made me understand some new aspect of it, some extra layer. It struck me that maybe this was how the people of a place went to work on you as you yourself lived in, or through, or with it – each piece of their past that you came to learn, each story from their present that you played some small part in, each hope for their future that you were made somehow aware of, all fed into your own ever-expanding perception and comprehension of this specific patch of earth in this specific period of time. And perhaps there was something in the accumulation of contact that might generate that deepening of comprehension – that what began as something thin, something at the surface of things – a banal conversation made up of clichés, had eventually accumulated specifics and richnesses, an authentic reality, through time and repetition, deep feelings and thought. And so, for instance, Ron found, through their slowly evolving interactions, that Tom's Irishness (for that is one important way that Tom perceived himself, although he moved to the village at the age of five and had no trace of an accent), was not quite the same Irishness he thought of when he'd applied for his passport, or that he used in his awful, old-fashioned jokes, or indeed the same Irishness he had once seen in the prohibitive signs in the pubs of his own youth. He certainly started to think of 'the Irishman' in his jokes and Tom as having separate meanings, somehow. It would be impossible, I imagined, to articulate any of this to Ron, who continued, despite that growing inward sense, to want to make those jokes and who, if he was ever pulled up on a point of politically correct etiquette, quickly bemoaned a culture which he thought, despite the evidence in front of his eyes – in the column inches and headlines in the *Daily Mail* that he would leave behind him in the pub most nights for us to ceremonially put on the fire – was conspiring to stop people 'like him' speaking what he thought of, rightly or wrongly, as 'his mind'. For my part, I thought of my walks along these paths, about how the hills behind the rooftops on the high street changed across the hours, days, weeks, months, across the seasons and years, and how, finally, they came to be something so burningly alive, so unique and powerful and intensely real that at times I could hardly bear to look up at them, or be out under their canopy or sharing their luminous green light. They grew in my imagination until the word 'hill' could not contain them.

* * * *

At the bottom of the high street, at what was referred to (rather unfairly it seemed to me) in the 1976 Countryside Commission Long-Distance Footpath Guide to the Ridgeway as an 'ugly clock tower', I turned right and walked up the Tring road, past a little row of thatched cottages known colloquially as Anne Boleyn Cottages, supposedly a wedding gift from Henry VIII. Hollyhocks struggled with the wind in one or two of the little front yards, another was filled with lavender, another a couple of small rose bushes. Outside the cottages, lining the roads, expensive cars shone in the early morning sun. An Audi, a BMW, an Aston Martin. On the opposite side of the road was a long track that led up to the main farm in the village. A little way down the track an old farmhouse sat among barns and various work vehicles. Tractors and pickups and quad bikes. A rainbow flag drifted in and out of life at the top of the flagpole which stood outside one of the large outbuildings. These rainbows had been displayed in windows and gardens across the country during the lockdown as a kind of symbolic show of gratitude and support for the NHS workers during the pandemic. I also noted that day that it was, perhaps coincidentally, the week of the Pride festivities in London, or would have been under normal circumstances. There was always the chance that this coincidence had crossed this particular farmer's mind. He had a colourful history of his own – a reputation as being larger than life, a benign troublemaker, a local trickster. He had been somewhat of a hedonist in his younger days, an avid attender of gigs, raves, a devotee of the early super-clubs. I recalled a conversation I had with him just before the last general election in the queue for the Post Office, when, and this despite his current public show of affection for the NHS, he had said the prospect of a Corbyn-led Labour victory – your lot, he had said to me – would be a bloody communist disaster. In the weeks after the EU referendum, he flew a huge EU flag from his flagpole, and I remember him saying in the pub that he didn't really give a shit about the funding, about the loss of subsidies, or how he might be better off outside the EU or inside it, or whether he could now export his lamb to bloody Timbuktu, all he really cared about was that he was worried it'd be a royal pain in the arse for him to fly his little plane over to France for the day for lunch. The farmer had known my mother since they were children in the village, and my father since he moved here with my mother all those years ago. When they arrived here to start running the Lantern, the farmer had not yet fully taken on the responsibilities and workload of what was then still his father's farm and was at leisure to raise merry, if rather parochial, hell. He would let off fireworks on New Year's Eve down at the clock tower, giddily drive his sheep flock down the high street, holding up traffic. His younger brother, who would of course be spared the eventual pressures and privileges of inheritance, owned one of the other pubs in the village called the White Water Inn which stood away past the church and off the road to London. It was a little walk to get there, up a long, tree-lined road that once led out to the main well and the source of the little chalk stream that gave the village and the pub its name. In the years of the farmer's younger brother's stewardship, the place accumulated a large and scandalous local legend – it had a back room which had been used for live music, discos, club nights – in fact all sorts of money-spinning, custom-generating, and eventually eyebrow-raising activities. The envelope was pushed perhaps just a little too far by the endmost use of the back room as a kind of pop-up adult venue on otherwise dead Sunday afternoons, with the regular arrival of strippers and burlesque performers presumably causing no little consternation among the residents of the quaint cottages that were to be found nearby. The pub was out of the way, but not quite isolated enough for the entrepreneurial extravagance of its owner, who eventually fell foul of the authorities and had the rare misfortune of losing not only his own licence but also that of the building itself, which was eventually turned into a drab set of offices. In the village the court case still came up now and then in conversation, the pub and its heyday fully enshrined in legend, and with no little amusement at the memory of the worthies of the village – the gentlemen farmers of the old school, the prim teachers, the eminent bankers and wealthy estate agents, the respectable, the hard-working – having to sit through proceedings that were, by all accounts, extremely detailed in their recounting of the various debauches that the pub had played host to over the preceding few years. The younger brother moved away to France once the pub had closed and was occasionally seen visiting the old farm. I had a great deal of time for the farmer one way or another. He was bullish and energetic and sanguine. He had a presence that was ridiculous and hopeful and happy.

Past the cottages and up over the top of the hill, I cut across the road and up into the first line of houses on the estate. Front gardens with their wooden gates, a toy tricycle outside one, more lavender, more lawn. The final house on this row was another that I remembered well from my childhood. A square brick building with a square front yard and, as I recalled it, a small back garden. The front door was now a bright royal blue, but when John lived there it had been a pale green. John was the third of our group. We had, the three of us, been in the same class in the local middle school before Stephen and I went off to the grammar, and John to the secondary modern there in the village. The three of us had, however, remained close friends throughout those school years. John's parents were defined, to my mind at least, by very different qualities to Stephen's. Where Stephen's were gregarious, sociable, outgoing, John's were quiet, hermetic. There was some quality about them that seemed to come from a different age. They seemed older, not necessarily as individuals, but rather as a whole, as an aesthetic, as an ethical and spiritual proposition. There was something pre-internet about them. Their clothes, their voices, the decorative decisions they had made in their home, their manners, their bearing. They had lived in the village all their lives, and so had their parents and their parents' parents. They were a devoutly religious and musical family, and although their house was modestly sized, there was a piano in the front room, an acoustic guitar always in its stand in the corner, harmonicas on the side, an accordion behind the couch.

Our friendship was, I suppose, in some ways rather peculiar, given that generally, as the children of the

village went through the process of 'selection' for the
secondary stage of their education, via the 11-plus
exam, so they also went through a kind of social
selection. Did I really remember noticing some new
mood in the school the very day after we had all got
our results? Or was it the case that I had overlaid my
own subsequent and long-held thoughts and feelings
onto the memory of that day? I had heard parents
in the pub over the years defend the principle of the
exam. I'd heard the old men at the bar talk about
meritocracy and 'simple' fair play. Everyone takes the
same test, everyone has the same chances. Nonsense
of course – the tests are as different as the children
themselves. The test is no more absolute, no more
objective, than any other experience. I can remember
nothing about any of the tests I myself took. Even at
that time, though, I remember thinking how grubby
the whole thing felt. How we had been sold, and had
indeed bought in, seemingly overnight, and as young
children, to this article of faith, to this one moment
of our lives that had taken on the weight of myth and
that might guild or blight our remaining days.

There were the adults who insisted it didn't matter
– teachers and parents. And yet you could see how
it infected each one of our lives from the very next
morning, and how as adults nobody could ever quite
let the whole process go. From time to time I thought
how ridiculous the parents of the latest batch of
kids to take the test sounded in the pub, sometimes

months, a year, two, after the fact, discussing the mistakes that had evidently been made, how their son or daughter had so obviously been placed at the wrong school. I remembered once when two couples were talking about a boy from their children's year who had, apparently, arrived in the village only a few weeks before the exam. He'd had no private tutoring, no preparation, no past papers. He'd started at the middle school because his father had moved in with a girl from the village. His three and her two – five kids in the house, for Christ's sake, one of the men said. I listened to them make their jokes about the father's job, about the kids' names. It turned out that this child, the latecomer with no special training for it, passed the exam with one of the highest grades in the year. These other parents took it personally that this kid had not had to do what it seemed to them they should all have had to do. He, or more accurately his parents, hadn't done things quite by the book. Of course these kinds of conversation carried on through the whole process of education, one year and one cohort after the next – I heard them when it came to the GCSEs, then the A Levels, then the subtle boasts and passive-aggressive preening that came with which universities the children all went off to. And I remembered it all from my own time. How it numbed me, in some way, this sense that I gleaned from the teachers and parents that we were bound up in the whole performance. Before she found herself with five children in the house, back when she only had the two of her own, that girl used to get in the Lantern now and then. I thought about talking to her a couple of times, and in fact still did, though she rarely came in much anymore. Precisely what I would have said to her, of course, I do not know. How brave were those words of the complicit grown-ups too, to talk about the opportunities afforded every child in the school, regardless of the result. But it was for the children themselves to take the test and to subject themselves to the hard binary of success or disaster, pass or fail, bright or dim. And the myth was the same as that which infected the whole country, the whole economy – that there was any such thing as merit. That any success, from this moment right through their adult lives, was down solely to ability or talent, and not secretly or substantially supplemented by the kind of luck that meant they found themselves being brought up in a household that could afford the time or the money to provide a private tutor, or a household that had books in it, or a household that spoke the language that the examination was written in. All this was the central, powerful lie, that held everyone in thrall in this place. These schools, this one year of exams in their children's and family's and friends' lives, shattered or stunted, or propped up each and every one of us.

Of the three of us, it was John who had been the real sportsman. He'd played all through his teenage years for the football club in the village, which was run out of a small, dilapidated clubhouse on the far field by the school. Nowadays the club was run by two brothers called Bruno and Renato who were around the same age as me. Their parents were Italian, the father a builder and well known and liked around the village. The brothers each supported a dfferent one of the two big Milan clubs, and had changed the club's strips so that the home jersey was red with black stripes and the away jersey blue with black stripes. They had both played for the club all their lives, and on occasion, especially on Saturdays after the game if they were in the pub, they argued as to which of them had accrued the most appearances, who had scored the better or more important goals, who had contibuted more or less to the team, and so, by implication, to the village itself. I remember once, when they were still quite young, that one of these arguments escalated into a full-blown fight. They ended up outside, fighting on a small patch of grass by the roundabout. A few of us had gone outside, to what purpose I could not now really say, perhaps simply to watch, or to break the fight up, perhaps to prevent anything serious from happening. Anyway, after a furious but ultimately tame scuffle, a police car arrived and one of the constables got out and pulled the pair apart. I don't remember really what he said to them, but I do remember Bruno, the eldest, offering up as his sole defence the fact that the two of them were, in fact, brothers. To our amusement, the constable actually seemed to accept this as a valid reason to fight in

public, and as I recall it now, ended up driving the
two of them up the hill to the kebab van that used to
operate outside the RAF base on Friday and Saturday
nights to cater for the young cadets coming back up
the hill from the multitude, as there then were, of
village pubs.

Occasionally I would still go and watch the village
football team, partly out of my sense of attachment to
what was still, despite my long litany of frustrations
with it, my hometown, partly nostalgia for John.
I often recalled a match I attended a few years ago,
a pre-season friendly against a team from the town
called Aylesbury Asians. The village team's goalkeeper
at the time was a man who I saw in the pub quite
regularly – another Pete who everybody called Pete
the Posts. He was extremely short for a goalkeeper,
and so already attracted the eye, but he also wore
a thick beard that came a good way down his chest
and had extremely long, luxuriant, curly brown hair,
which flowed out from underneath the leather flat
cap he wore to keep goal in. This particular match,
the visiting team had brought a few spectators with
them – family, friends and a number of children.
These children assembled behind the home side's
goal, and we could all hear them begin to harangue
the unfortunate goalkeeper. What *is it*, though. What
is it? they shouted at him, his extravagant hair and
idiosyncratic style obviously arousing their interest.
They had soon excited themselves into that singular

state, almost exclusive to childhood, in which they had brought upon themselves a kind of manic delirium of laughter. They were in fits of hysterics, each taking it in turns to shout What *is it*, bruv? What is it? Is it a dwarf? Is it a midget? Is it a wizard? It's so *small*, bruv. And it must be a Muslim, one of them said, it's got a beard. The goalkeeper himself was trying desperately to keep an eye on the game, but would now and then attempt to shoo them away. I know what it is, one of the kids finally shouted, it's a *gnome*, mate. It's a gnome, like out the garden. They were uncontrollable by now in their laughter. And those of us in earshot could not help but be amused too. Eventually they grew bored and moved off. I think they began a game of their own away from the pitch. The match ended up as a one-all draw. Very creditable at the time, I thought, as I knew a few of the Aylesbury Asians players and they had a very useful side. The goalkeeper ended the game saving a penalty in the final minutes. A very good shot-stopper, Bruno always said, but he had great difficulties controlling his box at corners.

* * * *

At the end of what I still, even then, referred to in my mind as John's road I cut through a little alley and up into the woods that rose with the hillside behind the south-eastern edge of the village. These were the woods that were named for the village and covered the hill from here to the next nearest town along the ridge.

They were also the woods in which Stephen and John and I had spent so much time as children. In amongst the trees at this edge of the wood there were the remains of an Iron Age fort settlement, now a large earthwork ring, a jump for kids on their bikes, a point of interest on one of the chalkboards at the large and newly appointed visitor centre by the car park, which the Forestry Commission had spent so much of the previous year expanding. These woods had, since those pre-Roman times of the fort settlement, always been managed, or perhaps more accurately manhandled, the environment to a certain extent always built, or built upon. Charcoal-makers, bodgers, sawyers and pig-herders would all have left a discrete imprint of their own and much later, most notably during the two world wars, the woods were heavily felled to provide timber and replanted with conifers and Chinese maples. Now there was a café, public toilets, trail markers, a huge statue of a Gruffalo overlooking the valley to the east, a Go Ape centre with its attendant ropes and swings and pulleys in the trees and staff in hi-vis jackets. There were bridleways, mountain bike trails. Dog shit bins, picnic tables, permanent BBQ stations, a solitary bird hide hidden away like a dirty secret off one of the paths. Relations between the human and the forest had always been the story of these woods and they offered themselves, over the course of time, as classifications of their own kind, to history. Great houses, great families, war, commerce, technology. The hill at the back of the woods is called

Aston Hill, and from 1904 until 1925 was the site of a famous automobile speed hill climb. Success in the climb led to one driver, a certain Lionel Martin, to begin to build his own cars. There was a monument now at the roadside near the top of the hill, the inscription of which reads:

The Origin of Aston Martin

From 1904 to 1925 Aston Hill, part of the Lord Rothschild's Estate, was a renowned motoring venue.

Lionel Martin made his first ascent of this hill in a tuned Singer Car on 4 April 1914.

Shortly afterwards, on the 16th May, at the Herts County Automobile & Aero Club meeting, he was so successful that in March the following year the sporting light car club first registered a car in his name called an 'Aston-Martin'.

It was the start of a legend in the history of the automobile.

This plaque was placed here by the Aston Martin Owners Club and Aston Martin Lagonda Limited.

I thought of that plaque whenever I saw one of those cars in the village. Perhaps there was one in the pub car park of an evening, or perhaps I would see one cruise down the high street and think of these ways in which we constantly rub up against the material facts of the past, more often than not without ever knowing it. You could have driven through this village, in your Aston Martin, and thought nothing of the hill away to the east. You would have left by the road that passed the track that led up to Aston Hill and the monument to that peculiar point in history that has, in its turn, led to this, to you and your car, here on the road. And yet that point in the past had no foreknowledge of you, could not know anything of this journey you now found yourself on – the journey to London, or the airport, or the coast. Your destination would never have been here, though, not this village, despite your strange links across time. There would have been no reason for it to be, for nothing that you saw in the village as you drove through had the appearance of mattering very much at all. You noticed nothing. Another little market high street. Another hill. Another wood. The village, and countless others like it, passed you by until you arrived where you were going. Wherever that was. Perhaps you were simply going home.

PART THREE

The Names and Their Cancellations

I decided, on a whim, I suppose, to take the towpath west and walk all the way to the main town nearby. This was the county town, the conurbation to which we had given the epithet 'town' when we were growing up, and where Stephen and I had gone to grammar school. Later it became where we went to try and meet girls but more often found ourselves in fights. It was a sad old concrete mess. Desultory – ruined by bad planning and disastrous architecture. There were some attractive buildings in what was called the old town, and a large market square which still carried some vestige of its once pleasant-looking past, but around that had been built a couple of ugly shopping centres and a brutal-looking concrete bus station, grey and dark and depressing. This part of the town, the

bus centre and a concrete underpass leading down
to the train station, had once been used as a set on
Stanley Kubrick's *Clockwork Orange*, but apparently
the scenes filmed here never made the final cut.
The joke was that they were too bleak even for the
purposes of that film, though there was something of
its hard malevolence in the underpass, in the ominous
cruelty of the council building. In fact, growing up
around here the town had always conveyed, in some
obscure way, its own undercurrent of suburban
violence. This was not entirely to do with the human
tensions that ran through the place, either – though
there certainly was a rubbing up of extreme poverty
and extreme wealth. Even if I could still now imagine
the array of first cars that had been driven by some of
the boys at our school – a little Mercedes sports car,
a Toyota Land Cruiser, a couple of flashy VW Golf
GTIs, I could also remember the run-down estates at
the edges of the town, the mostly empty retail spaces
that ran along the sides of the market square. Coffee
shop chains. Pound shops. Hidden away down the side
streets there were Polish supermarkets, Asian grocers
and dozens of kebab shops. But there was, as I say,
something else in the atmosphere of the town, and
in many others of a similar sort, no doubt. A kind of
listless, incoherent anger – an anger borne of boredom
and young manhood and which spilled out in the pubs
and bars at the weekends, or on the Sunday morning
football fields. There was a note of it in every over-
revved car engine. It was kept under manners at the

rugby clubs, turned into code and choreographed, but it was present there too nonetheless.

I headed away from the village where the canal meets the street that leads up to the school. In the time before the virus this would have been another parade of expensive cars dropping off kids that live within easy walking distance. The pavement full of parents standing around and catching up, or those that didn't drive them in would be riding their children's scooters back home for them, perhaps one or two preferring instead to carry them to avoid risking a fall. When I turned off the road and onto the towpath, I became aware again of the lack of the life of the school. The first five hundred yards or so of this path would normally be accompanied by the frenzied, high-pitched white noise of kids playing, but today the air seemed markedly devoid of those human sounds. I had never realised the nature of my response to that noise before, but in its absence now I came to feel that there was something freighted with life about it, all energy, ecstasy. It was as if it were at a kind of breaking point, at times, the sheer exultant joy in the pitch of their screams and shouts. I could imagine them now, running and running without fatigue for their fifteen-minute break or the short period of play they had before the first bell rang and they were confined to the classroom. It was my own childhood I imagined, of course, my own play and uniform and friendships, my own desperation on days like this of being stuck indoors, and the pure deliverance of the moment the doors opened, my legs broke into a run, and the playing fields passed underneath me, wide as the whole world.

This part of the canal was broad and reedy with a dozen or so female mallard in permanent residence, fed mostly on sliced white bread, or perhaps more likely these days, stale sourdough from the artisan baker's stall on the market. I walked on past the school's playing fields, past the little bridge that marked where the old small-gauge railway had once crossed the canal, and where as kids we would cross the water via the broken-up concrete and bits of rubble which were all that remained of the long since blown-up bridge. Bullhead and stickleback in the stony shallows. A buzzard called and I looked up to see it, quite close, circling above me in yet another clear sky. A female mallard cocked her head to the left, as if to allow that one particular eye to look up towards the raptor above. The buzzard kept on calling, and slowly circled away across the valley. I walked past the RAF sports ground, where a dozen or so crows sat on the immaculate green of the rugby and football pitches, and where signs told me I was not permitted to go. A green woodpecker took off from the grass, unaware of notions of permission or access, and bobbed its way into a group of ash trees up ahead. I passed the limits of the MOD land, the last of their signs warning against trespassing on military property, and carried on to where a row of bungalows had been built on the other side of the bank. A couple of them, it seemed, were having their back gardens, which ran right up to the water's edge, landscaped. All summer I had seen evidence of these kind of improvements – in the driveways and front gardens of the village bags of earth, compost and gravel had been proof of how things really stood out here during the lockdown measures. Time on people's hands, an opportunity to scrub up, to make good. I had heard people talking of a boom in the housing market in locations like ours, just outside of London, when people were allowed to move house again – of people leaving the city in case of future pandemics and lockdowns, moving where they had gardens and space and hills to walk in. So now was the time, quite obviously, to decorate the spare fourth bedroom, to spruce up the front drive, to put in a summer house, to hopefully add a few thousand on the asking price.

There was an enviable quality about living this close to the water and its relative abundance of life. On the opposite side of the bank, and so perhaps the dominant feature of the view from these houses, was a huge and overbearing field that sloped up into the base of the hill line, where it was separated by the Tring road. The field would stink of shit come autumn, when it would be fertilised with manure. In the dark months of winter it would loom over the houses, the hills in the background black against a pale sky, the

field sodden and brown, the greens of summer all
but impossible to recall in the pinched, grim days of
that season. But today, let it be said, the field rolled
away from the eye and up to the road, with an almost
pastoral, painterly aspect. Approaching the road
bridge that marked the leaving of our village and the
entering of the next, I heard a disturbance from the
foliage down by the water and stood and watched a
brown rodent with a pale tail slip into the water beside
me and swim across the canal. It slithered fast out and
up into the reeds on the other bank. Underwater, the
animal was too obscure to identify with any certainty,
but given the perilous state of water vole populations,
and my own downbeat mood, I concluded it must
have been a rat and moved on. What did it say about
me, about my desires for these walks of mine, for the
interactions that I longed for, that I had established
an unconscious hierarchy of things within my own
head, a table of abstract values attached to certain
species and not to others? I took my little tick-list with
me wherever I went – the things I took most pleasure
in observing. Kingfisher, little grebe, grey heron,
sparrowhawk, jay, green woodpecker. This wasn't a
simple matter of rarity, but something else. It was
as if certain properties animated my experience in
different ways. I had once tried to explain how I felt
to Stephen, who had a cooler, more phlegmatic way
of seeing. As always, I could not quite pin down with
language all that I was trying to say, or feel. Even
now I knew that a water vole would have brought on a

feeling of a very different kind to that of a rat – but I
could not really say why, or even with certainty which
of the two I had just seen. And what, in the end, did it
matter which it was, for was that animal not a single
living thing, no more or less common than any other, a
single life in opposition to any group I wished to claim
it for. The rat should mean no less to me than should
anything else that crossed my path that day. In fact,
I decided, the thing had been of great value, for it had
sharpened my wits and my eyes. I would approach
every living thing I saw that day with a renewed sense
of longing, of avidity for the world. Of course, as I
thought these things, I was at the same time aware
of just how artificial the feelings would necessarily
be. I had made myself believe, through the intricacies
and convolutions of my constant internal arguments,
that my feelings should tend a certain way, that I
should look, and understand things through a certain
sensibility. Did nothing come naturally to me? Was
everything the result of wrangling and chastisement?
Of knowledge and the denial of knowledge? Of the
'names and their cancellations', as Tim Lilburn had
it? Wren, treecreeper, wood pigeon, wood pigeon,
rook, rook, rook.

Where the canal bed began to run dry, there was a
series of wooden bridges, each of which was covered
with small plaques of dedication to people I supposed
had donated time or money in support of the project
that had been underway for a good dozen or so years

to restore this arm of the canal. Each time I passed
them, I stopped for a moment and made a point of
looking specifically for two of the plaques. The first
I tried to find was the one dedicated to the patron of
the project, a famous actor, well known to the whole
country, though with no connection to the village and
its stretch of obsolete waterway. It always amused me
to see his name there among the others. Of course, I
knew absolutely nothing about the man and he may,
for all I know, be an enthusiastic supporter of canal
restoration projects across the country. Nevertheless
I found the idea of him, especially imagined through
the persona of his most famous character (the
character for which he was so well regarded – a
pompous snob and a foreigner who regularly came
up against the ignorance of fictional versions of this
kind of little England), knowing of the existence of
this little wooden bridge on a long-forgotten arm of
canal always felt somehow implausible. It felt like
a thin place between the two realms – the fictional
and the real, the actor and character, the nature of
a real village and its equivalent tropes in its long
line of representations and misrepresentations. The
other plaque I always looked for had the name of
one of the Lantern's regulars on it – another one of
our many Petes. He was a prison guard in the town,
and so had quite properly been given the nickname
'Porridge' by the same young woman, in fact, who had
been involved in the argument at the open mic. Pete
Porridge came in mostly very early, always dressed in

his walking clothes, which were of the sort that had a vaguely military feel – two chest pockets, epaulettes on the shoulders, shades of khaki. Occasionally he would come in after work, still in his uniform. His white shirt immaculately ironed and unmarked. He drank real ale and sat at the bar. He was another crossworder, but where Monkey Wrench Mark used the newspapers the pub took, Pete Porridge always brought in his own *Telegraph*. He had a strange and singular way about him, a quality that was innately likeable though for reasons one could never fully comprehend. His conversation, for instance, did not sparkle. He was neither specularly well-read or informed, he'd not lived a storied or glamorous life. He had a complete disinterest in culture of any kind – he showed no capacity for books, for art, and most pointedly he had a deep suspicion of the contemporary obsession with sport, which he thought brash and Americanised. Too much money, too many adverts. When he was young, however, he had been a keen bodybuilder, and my mother remembered him as having exhibited in a few local shows. She said it had always seemed odd now to see him in his guard's uniform, a somewhat grumbling presence though always quick to laugh, to remember him on stage in the Memorial Hall one night wearing nothing but a tiny pair of silk trunks, posing his musculature in those formal, almost architectural positions. To know him now, the idea of performance of any kind would seem wholly improbable. He was a man of no outward

extravagance – his clothes tending always towards
the invisible, the inconspicuous, towards something
like uniform. His choice of car was practical rather
than showy, his world was pragmatic and customarily
kept itself to itself. Perhaps it would seem, from this
description, that he was a hard man to like and yet
he was a favourite of both mine and my parents. How
could it be that, had I seen it written down, or heard
it second-hand, I could despise or, worse, be bored
by almost everything that came out of this man's
mouth and yet for all that find myself very much
liking him? Looking forward, even, to seeing him at
his stool, nodding at me or quietly slipping me his
glass for a refill. It occurred to me then that this was
the reason I always looked for his plaque. It had a
very simple dedication, just his and his wife's name,
but I believed it to be the communication of another,
mostly unseen aspect of the man. His occasional
and rather worn-out jokes, jokes delivered with just
the barest hint of conviction, about marriage and
domestic life – who can say what motivated them,
aside from the well of misanthropy that lay deep
beneath so much of what passed for humour in the
barrooms of middle England, all those ill-formed,
received ideas that had been passed around for
generations without question. This was something
essentially irredeemable, of course, but when I found
myself looking at their plaque I wondered if perhaps
he simply could not form into words, perhaps even
discern, the truth of his feelings towards his wife as

she was in the world, uncoupled from his ideas about womanhood and domesticity in general. This small dedication was his poem, his attempt to say what was beyond saying. Whatever it was that compelled me, I could never stop myself from pausing here in some strange homage to Porridge, and also taking in the other names and messages that adorned the bridge, the marks and titles and scraps of language that memorialised people, behind which lay an almost infinite living truth.

In places, the dried bed had taken on the character of the grassland that surrounded the canal – short grasses, thistles, nettles and knotweed had all grown up in a kind of sunken meadow. For longer stretches, however, the bed was nothing more than a pale, hard, cracked clay. Here and there were caterpillar tracks and bricks. Boot marks and palette boards, tools at rest. Evidence of yet more work, where the land still offered up signs of what had once been its function. I cut off the towpath and across a road, down a tight little footpath that led to one of the large reservoirs which marked the point at which I was to leave the unnavigable arm of the canal and cut back across the valley on the arm which took you into the town. I sat in a bird hide on the bank for a few minutes and ate a sandwich. I watched a handful of young black-headed gulls glide listless on the water. More mallard, great crested grebe, two mute swans. This particular section of the reservoir was a stocked trout water and

I watched a man and a woman throw out a few casts from their little punt. Their fly lines arched behind them in that perfect enactment of physics, of gathered energy and its poise and release, snapping into the forward thrust of the cast and out across the water towards, perhaps, a rise out on the surface that they were aiming for. I could have stayed and watched for hours, mimicking the couple's own patience, waiting in my own way for their bite, for that matchless exhilaration of the moment the fly is taken and the wrist cocks into the strike. But I had more miles to go to get into the town and so I went on, leaving them to their dreams of a huge rainbow or two.

I crossed the footpath onto the larger body of water just to the north and continued around the bank. Grey wagtails flicked themselves along the rocks at the water's edge, tufted ducks and dozens of coots cruised slowly on the dark water that somehow, perhaps through its colour, communicated its ominous, cold depth. A single Aylesbury duck fed on the green scum that had accrued at the base of one of the artificial islands that had been built out on the water. Two cormorants sat on the other, quite apart it seemed to me, watching the other birds, looking for all the world like memories or artefacts, out of their collective avian past. At the head of the reservoir, I climbed down a grassy bank and back onto the joining Aylesbury arm of the canal. Past a couple of locks and under a bridge where the towpath split, I took the path to my left, heading almost exactly west across the county and towards the town.

After a short while walking along this stretch, the trees either side of the towpath thinned to nothing, and away to both sides I could see out across the relentless, flat, empty-looking farmland of the vale. To the south I looked back in the direction of the village I had come from, the line of hills almost black against the horizon. A kestrel flew up from a half-fallen signpost in a yard across the water, and every now and then I was joined by small groups of martins that seemed to appear in the sky above me from nowhere. At some point I passed the last boat I would see until I came close to the town. It was hard to shake the feeling, as I walked these towpaths, that I was interacting physically with a system of travel and of engineering that had once transformed the whole of society. There was still, all these years after the fact, some impression of the limitless possibilities these waterways had once suggested. The disused boatyards, the two or three old hulks being worked on for nothing more than a way to pass the time, it was hard to picture the technology as it must have once seemed – utterly new and revolutionary, and yet the sense remained palpable somehow. It seemed at once improbable and self-evident, the scene still redolent of travel and commerce and the shrinking of space and time that industrialisation must have meant for those who crested its waves despite its atmosphere of obsolescence and oil-soaked depression.The canal was everywhere littered with signs of its past, long since abandoned. Then again even now the waterways cultivated a kind of shadow commercial and social population – a community with what seemed to me at least like a culture of their own. I remembered Pete Porridge once in the pub, bemoaning some slight despoiling of a bit of grass on the side of the canal by someone spilling motor oil, using the name 'canal gypos' to describe the people who lived on these boats. And it was true that along the towpath I occasionally saw parts of a motor spread out on a tarpaulin to be mended, or bits of a bicycle, or a strimmer, or a wheelbarrow. Nothing of the boats or their accumulated stuff seemed new – it all seemed old, well-used, lived-in and repaired, weathered, made to last. It seemed to me a way of living that was antithetical to the sustained consumption of new things that pervaded, indeed perhaps corrupted, those of us in the village. A kind of argument against the endless new cars and new bikes and new dogs and new phones that were always on display.

With that particular suddenness of movement that is so characteristic of encounters with the animal world, caught, somehow, from the very edge of what is in sight, I spotted a sleek black shape slip from the surface and come to rest at the foot of a neat little garden on the opposite bank. There were a couple of steps down to the water's edge and the long, dark shape crouched low to the brickwork of the last of them. I stopped and watched it for a few moments, motionless, before it stretched out to its full length along the step and very quickly, silently, ran away from me up through the shrubbery and into the garden. It was the first of its kind I had ever come across on the canal, an American mink. How strange that I should have wondered, just an hour or so previously, whether I had seen a water vole, and that I had thought about the implications and the meanings of the rarity of that species, only to here be confronted, quite by chance, and for the very first time, with a kind of animalistic emblem of one of the very reasons, or so I had read, for the vole's precarious position. In point of fact I felt exactly the same exhilaration at this small interaction as I would with any new or rarely seen creature. I exulted in this small invader, this fierce savage once skinned for its fur and now bringing a violence of its own to bear on the world. Who could hate any of these things, I thought, though it was also true that some long-held balance had been broken and the world, both of the canal here, and in its widest, planetary, deep-temporal sense, was reeling from it.

As I reached the outskirts of the town the buildings on either side of the banks began to build up, the evidence of human habitation began to accrue. Litter and muck. The water had grown an oily sheen. All around this town, making up its outer limits were small industrial estates, some converted now to retail parks full of brands like B&Q, Homebase, Sports Direct.

Horrible, big stores full of white light and mostly cheap, throwaway crap. Those that had not been changed in this way housed factories of various kinds. I thought to myself how they, too, must all be closed now. The instruments and tools and engines all still and silent, the vending machines half-empty, the canteens all clean and quiet. After leaving school, during both the summer before my aborted few weeks at university, and for the years after, while my friends did their degrees and lived their lives in the big towns and cities, I had instead done the rounds of these factories taking temporary work. I had, since, thought about whether that time was the reason I had carried such mistrust, such antipathy, towards work with me through life. No matter what I had done, it had all seemed so pointless, so futile. It never seemed to end. The line carried on all day, all week, all month. It became mantric, religious, ritualistic, powerful. The line was the machinery of time both invoked and overcome. The potential of my days was crushed at my picking station. A task with no finishing point, nowhere to get to, no point of completion. I worked in a factory that made and packaged up powdered soups and milkshakes, I worked in a salad factory making sandwich fillings. I opened five-litre cans of tuna one after the other, the brine sloshing all over my wellington boots, or I mixed the fish meat with mayonnaise in huge, industrial quantities, or I stood for hours at a centrifuge, separating the swarf that had sluiced off the metal turning machines from its oil, or I packed boxes full of CDs and DVDs with inflatable protective packaging, and booted the boxes around in the back of the lorry that came to collect them each afternoon, for no reason that we could discern aside from the easy, spiteful joy of the act. A wanton destruction of worthless pieces of plastic that matched the degraded circumstances of our daily lives. I had worked in an ice cream cone factory, dipping the cones into a vat of cheap, constantly boiling hot chocolate for eight hours a day. At that last place I had at the very least known one other person who was working there, a friend of John's from school who I had also come to know a little bit. One afternoon he came past my station on the line and removed the face mask he had to wear to cover his beard. His jaw was rocking back and forth seemingly of its own volition. I've taken rather a lot of ecstasy, he told me. Would I like some? I took a tablet off him, bit it in half and swallowed. That particular afternoon, I am bound to admit, passed much faster and more pleasingly than most. I took the other half straight after my shift and walked the four miles home in a blissful daze. I was not so high that the tilt or colours or sounds of the earth altered themselves as I took them in, not so high as to suddenly and powerfully understand some new conception of reality, or some new dimension of truth. It was just a gentle high, a softening at my own edges, my feet padding the ground a little gentler, somehow, as I walked back along the road.

Eventually, sometime later that year, I ended up working for the window cleaner in the village. Saved

at last, courtesy of happenstance and a conversation
in the Lantern one evening, from the crushing tedium
of the factories. The work was no less mundane,
I don't suppose, but the window cleaner's company
was at least interesting and the days passed as well as
I thought days might do. The window cleaner, who, it
should come as no surprise to find out, was called Pete,
had long been a regular in the pub, along with his two
brothers. Their surname was King and so everyone
naturally referred to them, whenever they came up
in conversation, as 'We Three Kings'. The window
cleaner was in fact rather well known around the area,
because for a couple of years, and this was some time
ago now, he had circumnavigated an inconvenient
ban he had incurred for drink driving by taking to
his round on a horse and cart. Unfortunately, he was
back behind the wheel of his beloved Citroën by the
time I was his help, and so I missed the opportunity
of seeing the county from the vantage point of a trap.
For some reason, I was put in mind of all this, of the
history of my own often mundane employment, as I
listened to the news on the radio in those days of late
June, just as the lockdown was beginning to ease. One
could sense that behind each new measure, each new
freedom, as they were sometimes then rather darkly
referred to, lay the simple truth that the time had
come for us, the great mass of populace, to go back
to work. Some papers phrased it as bluntly as that,
and I certainly heard a few people around the village
muttering that enough was enough. Apparently it was

just too much to bear for some to see the proles and
the plebs and the painters and plumbers and factory
workers enjoying all this newly unencumbered time.
Things can't be said to be working, I understood them
to mean, until the people are back at work, which
was just to say they must forever be expanding their
spending power. Our time was not our own, and nor
was our money – it was already spent the moment it
came to us. On rent, on food, on bills, on cars, on train
travel. The lockdown had opened up the possibility of
a different way of being – working from home, even
working less, travelling less, consuming less petrol
and plastic and all manner of other stuff. We had all
better return to the drudgery of the old orthodoxies,
then, in order to keep the whole sorry mess afloat and
to quickly forget any nonsensical ideas we'd started to
have about how we might alternatively spend our days
on earth. The banks, the builders, the speculators,
the big infrastructural projects, they all needed
people back in their proper positions. In fact none of
it meant anything more than a few cheap sandwiches
or a barrel or two of beer. The veneer of our culture
of work, of its own hierarchies and categorisations,
its long-held classes, grades and their statuses, had
been eroded. The lustre had gone. We squatted in
the channel, suddenly aware of what a shabby little
shithole we really were, all our qualities squandered,
all the sordid truth of our history laid bare. Any
humanity there might have been in the act of work
itself, any sense of its heroic function, had been

drained away. I read in one newspaper of humans being called 'market units'. Who could quantify the violence in that act of naming? But what did I do about any of this, anyway? Wrote my own shabbiness into mediocre poems and stood in silence behind the bar while the old men raged, incoherent, at the changes they perceived. Nothing, in short. As always, I did nothing.

The canal ran along the southern edge of the town, running slightly south-west past what had once been a large brewery but was now the recently developed site of a new theatre, the Bucks University campus, a big branch of Waitrose and the terminal point of the canal at the Aylesbury basin. A short distance before I came to the basin, I came up off the towpath and onto a small bridge made of red bricks. The bridge crossed the canal and led onto a small paved footpath that ran into the town to the north and back down towards my old school to the south. I stopped on the bridge and looked down into the water below. The bridge was a sorry, ugly structure. For almost every person who walked across it every day it would mean nothing. It was utterly unremarkable. And yet for me it possessed a quality that I could barely put into words. It was under this bridge, almost exactly twenty-two years ago, that a police officer found John's body after what had by then been a three-day search. For the first of those days, once we had been told by his parents that John had not come home after a night out and that they were convinced something was not quite right, we had – me, Stephen, and Stephen's father – gone into town to try and find some sign of him. I recalled what felt like hour after hour walking around the various sections of the town – the various factories and industrial estates, the schools, the two Tesco superstores, the train and bus station, the three public parks. We looked in the industrial bins, in hedges, behind buildings. We found nothing.

As I stood there on the bridge that day, I could still feel, with all the same terrible intensity, the exact sensation I'd had when Stephen's mother had phoned to tell me the news that his body had finally been found. As I remembered it, I had crumpled to my knees on the ground and begun a fathomless, primal crying the second I had put down the phone. But if I thought about that moment now, it appeared, like so much of my past life, like nothing more than a posture – a scene with stage directions, lighting, props. And I wondered how it was that we could, at once, still access all those distant and debilitating sensations while at the same time doubt the veracity of our feelings, and our response to those feelings. How can we pass this strange kind of judgement on ourselves in hindsight, mistrust the motives of our own memories, at the same time knowing, beyond all doubt, that their essence still colours each day of our lives? Is there no end to the hardness with which we will deal with ourselves? Of the facts of the case, I need say very little. John had been out for the night with some friends and had, in that almost innocent way of things around that age, fallen into some petty violence with another gang of boys. John had been badly beaten and, so I read in the newspapers as I had not attended the court case, supposedly driven to a different bridge on the canal some miles out of the town, and dropped into the water where it was deep enough to drown him.

The gang was caught and convicted. The youngest was a boy of just fourteen. There was a profound, almost incredulous, sense of shock that ran through the whole village at the news. At the pitilessness of the act itself. One of their own, a boy of only seventeen, just out of school and about to embark on what would have surely been the real stuff of his life, had suddenly gone. People were angry and dismayed, even those who had barely been aware of the family prior to those events. There was a palpable, keen, widely felt empathy with John's parents, who had to live through their own grief played out as a kind of public undertaking. I could perceive other things too in the voices of parents, of teachers, of schoolfriends. There was an odd sense of glamour to it all – to the newspapers and TV crews. And I was aware of a strange blend of horror, of fascination and even a perverse kind of excitement in those I spoke to who had not perhaps known John well enough for any of that to be entirely obliterated by the unmitigated sensation of grief.

* * * *

I had seen nothing of Stephen and his parents, or of John's parents, in a number of years. After Stephen's two younger sisters both left home, his parents sold the house up in the hills and moved down to the coast, to a town near the New Forest where they had regularly taken the three of us on camping holidays. I had promised to visit, but never had, and eventually Stephen and I just stopped getting in touch with each other. I saw on the internet when he had married and had his first child. I sent him a message of congratulations on each of those occasions, but each time the correspondence lost energy after one or two notes to each other. We hadn't even bothered the last time with the platitudinous promise to get around to seeing each other. But perhaps, I thought now, that was as it should be. I would not have seen our friendship descend to the level of meaningless phrases, of some undermining of the importance of what had been before. John's parents, too, had eventually moved away. For a few years they sent a Christmas and a birthday card, and for a year or two after John died, I tried to visit and say hello whenever I walked past the house. In those often chaotic years straight after his death, though, I found it increasingly difficult to rouse myself for the visits. They hurt and I saw that hurt reflected in the faces of John's mother and father. The conversations became stilted and the silences seemed full of our terrible experience, our mutual knowledge of what the world might do to any of us at any moment. Of course as I grew older, I felt guilty for letting these small considerations slip. But I had let much else over the course of my life slip too, both the good and the bad, and there was always some excuse or other for not doing anything much at all. The thought of travelling, even to visit Stephen in Oxford, then London, became too much to bear and I suppose he eventually became fed up of being the one to make the effort.

In the early days of the lockdown, I read about people contacting long-forgotten or neglected friends, using the surreal events and circumstances of their lives as they now found them as grist to get in touch again after years of silence. Or perhaps even more hopefully, there were stories of grievances long held being put to one side amid the uncertainty and the preparation for a kind of grief nobody quite knew the nature of. This too seemed somehow out of my reach. I tried to imagine what I would say, how I would broach that first contact, but I could never find quite the right phrase. The words, as they came, felt flat or forced, or weighed down by my years of inertia and perhaps in the end what should rightly be called a callous laziness. What would I offer anyway? When I was eighteen or nineteen and I visited John's parents, it could be that I had still carried with me some of the potential, some of the vitality and promise of John's own youth as they had understood it. The idea of the two of us going off to university, coming home for the holidays, even quitting and settling into life around the village, may have functioned as some version of things as they had imagined they would be. Now I was simply a stranger to them. A middle-aged man. An almost-reminder. And had I not, weighed up honestly, wasted the life which John had never had the chance to make good on? I did not mean some kind of material waste, some calculation of value based on the accumulation of successes or failures. Rather I meant that I had some sense of everything that I thought and felt, even the shame and guilt which I was now describing, as a kind of attitude, as a mannerism, something constructed. But had I not lived all this, too. Had I not truly been angry and confused and fearful and lonely? And had I not written it all out, over and over again, in fact, in the hope that some of it was real enough to make that writing mean something and have the plasm and glimmer of something living, not simply the rearticulation of the things that I had read about in books. Books that I had not, it seemed to me then, even been able to discover for myself, but books that had been found for me, given to me – by my parents, by Stephen or his mother, or by any number of other people who had cosseted me and protected me and lied to me and failed me, as I had lied to and failed myself. Perhaps John's parents no longer thought about those days of the three of us together. Perhaps they thought only of John. What did those days of waking early and heading straight for the woods mean to them, after all, for they were the days they never knew. The days we spent at Stephen's house, or at the skateboard ramp in the park, or at the cricket nets, or the football club, or simply idling away our days down by the canal. The long, loose days that matched the long, loose limbs of our boyhoods. The long, loose days that matched our limbs.

I remember talking about the whole thing once, only a couple of years later, to an old man in the pub. For some reason, perhaps his, perhaps mine, he had been able to get me to talk about some of those feelings I had known at that time, and he told me the story of a young woman who had died in the village some forty or so years before. She had been found behind what was then an old petrol station, but was now a Chinese restaurant just outside the village. It had made the news as well, this case, he told me. They'd never found the killer, the old man said, but he remembered well how all sorts of people had come forward at the time to offer their opinion or their version of events to the police or to the papers or to the people in the pub. He described the village as having changed from a place of intensely felt privacy, of small families and individual households, of petty, silent grudges and old wounds, to a kind of hothouse of public spirit. By a strange coincidence, a few years later again, a film crew got in touch with my parents to ask if they could film a couple of interviews in the pub. They were making a TV series about unsolved murder cases in England and wanted to film one or two of the locals who remembered that case and perhaps do a piece to camera with the series presenter. The presenter was an actress who had made her name playing a criminal pathologist working on these types of what they called cold cases. Of course news got round the pub that 'someone off the telly' was going to be in and we'd never had a busier Tuesday. One or two of the old boys camped out all day and by closing time we had never seen them in a worse state. I thought frequently about these two historic acts of violence, the scale of the acts themselves, how personal and precise they were, held up against the broader, crushing, everyday violence of life – the world burning up and the seas rising. Murderers and victims both is what we all, in fact, will one day find ourselves to be.

* * * *

High summer, bright, early morning. The dog days of June. I felt some resolve rise in me to take a stand of some kind against my life. Against my inertia, against the world outside which I feared so much. Thankfully, the moment passed and the sensation slowly subsided. Now was not the time for action. There was still some small birdsong with the dawn. Hot sun on the back of my neck. My feet, one after the other, chasing down the hill paths. That is not to be forgotten. That is to be recorded.

* * * *

I came down the stairs one morning to find my father attending to a flooded cellar. The night had brought a violent summer storm, and our ancient and puny drains always struggled to cope with significant rainfall. I sat in the saloon bar with a cup of coffee and quite naturally avoided helping him. We had long since established in our relationship that I was not required to assist in these sorts of situations, where I would undoubtedly be worse than useless, and where my father's short temper would be brought to bear upon my all too evident shortcomings. I was altogether too clumsy in situations like that, and in fact perhaps around the poky old building in general. Always hitting my head, or knocking something over in the cellar. No, the old man would work on stoically and feel all the better for it afterwards. No point diluting his enjoyment.

I sat and read an article about the overnight rains bringing their by now regular degradation to what was one of the emblematic natural features of these hills – the chalk streams. The water companies, so I read, were allowed by law to discharge raw, untreated human sewage into the rivers in 'exceptional circumstances', one of which, under the terms of their licences, was extreme rainfall. As with almost all such regulation, the whole process was gamed or ignored, the terminology flexed in order for the private water companies to act as they wished so they might maximise profits. And why should they not, after all, when even senior politicians, even the nation's leader

himself, had only recently dismissed the concerns
of the environment as mere 'newt-counting'. This
was the contemptuous bluster with which all such
concerns were handled, as if to point out the cronyism
and duplicity of government agencies, of special
advisors' firms being handed big public contracts, of
shady tech companies handling voting data, or any
one of a seemingly infinite and daily number of other
examples was to be a perpetual child tugging on the
coat sleeve of the grown-ups asking why? We were
spoken to as if notions of fairness, of good faith, of
care, of accountability were aspects of some childish
aversion to the realities of political life. Idealism. Areas
and natural features of the landscape were given
designation, acronyms, status, but at the same time
they were actively, cynically, exploited or destroyed.
There were all sorts of well-meaning organisations
and societies dedicated to preserving this or that, but a
look at one specific body's work from the previous year
would reveal that the majority of the funding for one of
their big projects came from exactly the private water
company that had been found, in this area, to have
discharged untreated human shit into the water several
thousand times in the same year. But we go on, acting
out the vagaries of our conscience while the whole
mechanism of governance secretly and not-so-secretly
moves itself against us. Then again, the big climate
movements of the day appeared wary of ideologies that
might provoke scorn – or worse, ridicule. One of the
more infamous and renowned groups sought to distance

itself from words like 'socialism', claiming that their
organization had, in fact, no ideology, that they trusted
no single set of political ideas to find any better possible
futures. Not trusting in some alternative, it seemed to
me, was in effect to grant trust that the status quo and
all its machinery might somehow alter its own path.
I saw nothing of hope in that. In fact I saw an ideology
of its own – a kind of conservationism that was happy
enough with gestures but which lacked any true radical
ambition – an ideology of good marketing and 'content',
social media and arts events. In short, the same
language as that deployed by the water companies, the
government trusts, the fossil fuel energy providers or
any other profit-turning con men you cared to mention.
I despaired at all of it. I despaired and did nothing.

All this is not to say, of course, that to walk along one
of these chalk streams, to walk perhaps for a whole
day, along the length of a stretch of river that took you
from just inside the M25 all the way back here to the
village would not yield its own particular pleasure. It
is simply to say that this was how things stood. Care
should be taken, for instance, if you wished to swim.

I took the train, which had started to run once more
in and out of the capital from the village. I went as
far as the stop before the terminus at London and
walked back, where one could, along the course of a
chalk stream called the Chess. Disembarking from the
train, I walked downhill towards the town's centre,

which still carried some sense of dearth, although the lockdown measures had now eased. Perhaps it was simply fewer people, less of the hum of conversation, background music, traffic. A few people walked up the high street, a café was open and there were people sitting on the metal chairs outside, but the town hall and the library looked permanently, forbiddingly closed, the two pubs I passed looked as if they had been deserted for years. Was it some barely visible sediment of dust that gave away these buildings' indolence and inactivity, or some other aspect, passing outside the realm of our conscious, rational thought that told of the place's emptiness, its abandonment? I took a path that ran down the side of a large brick church and along past a cricket field. An old man on an old tractor pulled the sight screen across the outfield. By now the only birdsong was the characterful clicks of the jackdaws on the grass and a robin or two singing. The creep of winter's symbols into a set piece of high summer. A couple of plastic flags remained stuck in the ground after the weekend's games, and though the whole of July remained before us, I could feel in the image an intimation of autumn, of summer's end. The air that day, though, still had that high summer thickness, a breathless air of insects and the heavy, blended scent of plants. Perhaps it was that which anticipated the season's own demise. Everywhere the greens were outrageous, the foliage extravagant. There was an element of decadence, of opulence in every verge. The cricket field marked the edge of the town to the west, and the place where the path finally joined the river, which here in the town became a tributary of the larger river Colne. I travelled back the way I had just come, walking around the northern edge of the town, the river path taking me in almost the same direction as the railway line, and after about an hour's walking I came to a thin little path that ran for a short while alongside the M25 motorway before eventually crossing it. Huge rust-coloured metal sheets made a boundary fence and ran high up to where the road could be heard hissing and groaning above me. Little mammalian scrapings in the dirt every few yards, aborted attempts to breach the boundary. I crossed the motorway and picked up the river path on the other side, and slowly the suburban town and that road which also had the quality of a kind of outer boundary to the city gave way to country that would remain much the same for the long miles home. There was something about this movement beyond the M25 that felt meaningful to me in that moment. This slipping through the landscape and its different signs and modes of working, its different ways of occupying space, its different uses of itself, and of the human and the non-human. The archetypes of river and road, of moving back towards the solitude of my actual life from what I had come to see as the divergent existence I might have had in the city, but which, of course, I had long ago turned away from. These oppositions came too easily to mind, and should always be, if not rejected outright, then at the very least examined thoroughly.

The city and the country had always been co-opted, reduced to nothing more than thin, meaningless symbols that bore no resemblance to the true experience of either. Since before the EU referendum, for instance, you could find commentators who wanted to talk about London's distinct political sensibilities, its cultural hegemony, its ever-growing accumulation of everything from the nation's talent to its money. Walking in the opposite direction, away from the city and towards the very middle of England, I was put in mind of how the landscape as I saw it then was used in much the same way – how it was loaded up with a certain narrow sense of its own history to activate a set of feelings that might then be used by anyone from advertisers or shady online political pressure groups to actual foreign governments. We were a country in love with a rural conception of its past, its culture, its traditions, while also desiring the power and prestige of its industrial-urban self, its financial clout, its addiction to markets and status-wealth. They were confections, all of these myths we relied upon – they bore little relation to the bare facts of things which were in reality far stranger and wilder.

For long sections of the path, the river was nowhere to be seen, the track driving me away from its meanders, its banks, the noise of the motorway in the distance a double mockery – here I was, after all, walking a river path with no sign of a river and the sound of the cars and lorries and SUVs a mimic of the

rushing of water over stones. A little before I came to
a hamlet called Sarratt Bottom the river came back to
me and I crossed it at an old weir. On the brick bridge
I stopped and watched a few small trout holding
themselves hard against the gentle current, heads
absolutely still, tails tilling the moving water. Along
this part of the valley the fields had once been a large
system of watercress beds, and though there was still
one working cress farm here, they were now mostly
being grazed by horses. Here and there I saw a pool of
water on the surface, or a patch of lilies in the grass,
as if the field remembered the time when it belonged
to the realm of water. Once the industrial growing
and selling of watercress had thrived in this area,
but for the most part now the enterprise had become
just another historical anecdote, a point of interest
on a website or in a leaflet picked up from a library
or a ramshackle tourist information point in the clock
tower or town hall or church in any one of the villages
nearby. I crossed another marshy field and watched a
female kestrel sitting on top of a bleached tree stump.
Six cows sat in the shade of an oak. Not yet midday
and the heat was already oppressive. At the end of
the field the river had seemed to dry up to no more
than a muddy track but as I crossed the borders of
the grounds into the fields beyond it bubbled back
to life somewhere to my left, invisible aside from a
few glimpses through the thick growth at its banks.
Here the river bent round sharply to the west, and I
followed it past more disused cress beds, a small wood

away to the south and past a few attractive houses that had coalesced around a large farm.

At Latimer House, once a stately home of some note, but now a run-of-the-mill hotel and conference centre, and just as the building itself became visible on my right, so the land fell away sharply to my left and I could suddenly see the river once more, this time a good five hundred yards away, down at the bottom of the valley, fenced off to all but the two fly fishermen stood throwing casts from the banks, and of course the mute swans and Canada geese by the water's edge. Latimer House was not in any meaningful way the same building that had once been the prison of Charles I, and subsequently the refuge of Charles II, the original Elizabethan building having been mostly destroyed by a fire and so rebuilt – nonetheless it still carried, at least to me, that dual sense of both shelter and stronghold as I walked across its grounds. At the edge of the house's parkland, I was once again taken far up and away from the river, pulled by the footpath to circumnavigate a huge wheatfield. In the centre was a small copse of three or four old oaks. In the autumn, after the harvest, this field would be bare except for the pale flints which gave it an almost ghostly aura. The very size of it was peculiar, its long, luxurious curve down to the valley and the river below.

I have mentioned before my long uneasiness around dogs. Stephen's parents had a couple of spaniels

with which I slowly attained a mutual tolerance, but
I could not, for whatever reason, bring myself ever
to wholly relax around the animals. And perhaps it
is true that this unease communicates itself to the
creatures themselves in turn somehow, for they have
always acted in every way possible to augment or
confirm my own agitations. And here, at the end of a
long path across the bottom of a field, I found myself
facing off with a large black Labrador, no lead, its
owner nowhere to be seen, barking loudly and intently
at me and seeming to wish to guard, at all potential
cost to the hapless walker, the gate behind it. Of
course I turned and walked away, uphill along the
western edge of the field, sweating with the effort of
the incline, the dog's barking and howling echoing up
the field after me. By the time I got to the next turning
west, the direction I needed to head in, I was quite far
from my original route. It mattered very little, for the
footpaths had long since come to amount to the same
thing and in truth I was tired of them, whichever
direction they took me in. I trudged on however,
defeated and in low spirits, across the featureless
farmland until I reached the town where the river
rose, and to which the river had once given its name.

I chose to skirt the southernmost part of the town,
thus avoiding another haunted-looking market square,
its chain coffee shops just about open, its commerce
and character limping towards normality. I could walk
along the river for a short while and eventually join

the footpath that would climb and cross the hills and bring me back to the village. All day I had walked and all day I had felt harassed by the closeness of hedges and barbed-wire fences, by the sound of helicopters above me, by the incessant flicking of flies away from my face. The truth was that the walking had been miserable – pinched into little passageways and tracks or slogging over dull empty fields of arable crops. Now young brambles and sycamore saplings encroached on the paths which were hedged so tall that one walked with no view but the path ahead for yard after yard. Horseflies and horse shit. One farm after another. I felt as if the land and its boundaries were barely giving me room to breathe. As I continued, hemmed in on both sides, I began to hate the builders of these fences, convinced as I was that they had made each one as narrow as they could, grabbed every inch of land that they could possibly hope to justify.

After a few miles of walking away from the town and its outcrop of farms, the footpaths, for a while at least, opened out as I walked through a small wood at the foot of a row of huge gardens. I passed these and into more farmland. Two or three huge cornfields in a row stretched away from me to the horizon on either side, broken here or there by a single tree, or a cottage roof glimpsed over the curve of the land. Everything seemed lifeless. The sky was empty, the land gave no sound that might suggest a deer or a rabbit or a rat. I cannot speak for the thousands of tiny creatures

that were all around me going about the business of
living. Those beyond the boundaries of the everyday
human gaze, those without common names, beyond
our thought or imaginations. I did not as a matter of
fact feel as if I had been out into the country at all that
day. I felt as if I had been corralled across it. Driven.
All day I had walked alongside barbed wire, electric
fencing, conifer hedges, brambles. Helicopters above
me, my phone tracking my position, counting my
footsteps. Impossible to lose myself here in a country
as small and mean as this.

* * * *

On the internet one day I read that a skeleton had
been found in the archaeological excavations that
had been going on as part of the HS2 work in the
field to the north of the village. I read on a dedicated
website called 'HS2 in Bucks and Oxfordshire'
about the significant discoveries that the works had
facilitated. Not just the body, but also a large circular
timber monument, similar to Stonehenge. I read
also how this kind of archaeological work was almost
impossible without big infrastructural projects like
this one to piggyback on. In fact, a couple of years
before it had been reported that this would constitute
the biggest dig in the country's history, sixty or so
separate excavations along the length of the route as
the tunnel-boring machines did their work. It was yet
another example, or so I read, in language that was

almost pleading in its earnest representation of the co-operation between the juggernaut of HS2 and the archeological team involved, of notions of progress creating notions of opportunity. Growth and labour. These were the concepts that linked themselves through time, and each of which meant nothing without the other.

I continued to keep an eye on the protests just outside the village which were also in the news. Around the same time as the skeleton was discovered footage was leaked to news sources of HS2 contractors cutting a rope which was holding a protestor on a walkway suspended above a river. They fell twenty feet, hit the riverbed and were hospitalised. According to the website, the first thoughts of the geographers who had unearthed the skeleton were that it had also been the victim of an act of violence. The hands were bound and the body had been buried face down. Evidence of life in the area going back four thousand years. Four thousand years of burials and earthworks. Lives tracing themselves across time in patterns of travel and agriculture, tension, strife, violence. There were other patterns too, I began to think, as I learned more about the digs. There were some sections of the work being carried out on land that was not public. Further significant discoveries behind the stone walls that fenced off the private estates that most of us would never see, and perhaps the same would now be said of the things that were found there. Perhaps

all the knowledge, all the histories, all the treasures
that might yield themselves out of the land would be
hoarded in much the same way as that land itself had
been. That summer the way we had viewed the public
aspect of historical artefacts had been much discussed
– collections like those of Hans Sloane and Pitt Rivers,
collections which had been the foundation of national
archives and museums had suddenly come to the fore
as the country tried, belatedly, to bring some kind of
responsibility to bear on the violence and thuggery of
its past. Then again, in some quarters the very idea
of such a thing seemed preposterous. History was, for
them, perhaps simply the stories of an age long gone,
uncoupled from the present where the shame or guilt
was just too hard to bear, and yet strangely prescient
where strands of a culture or tradition could be put to
work for some spurious effect or other. I remembered a
year or two before when I had applied for a teaching job
at a local adult education centre. Part of the induction
process had been dedicated to something the centre
called 'British values', and it had sections with names
like 'fair play', 'democracy', 'tolerance'. I thought of
how at odds that sometimes seemed with the living
reality of the place as I knew it. I thought of the saloon
bar of the pub, for instance, and how those old boys
fought each day to preserve those values with their
casual dismissal of foreigners and foreign things. For
some reason the thought that struck me most hard
that particular morning was one of the more amusing
examples, such was its almost surreal stupidity.

I recalled a time when, sitting alone up at the bar, Pete
Porridge had ordered a bowl of chips for his lunch. He
was asked by Jim, who was working that afternoon,
if he had wanted any ketchup or anything else.
Mayonnaise, Jim had happened to mention, which had,
much to the amused surprise of those of us in the bar,
elicited the most incredible response. It would appear
that mayonnaise had, in some profound sense, been to
blame for almost all the ills visited down upon our great
nation since the moment when the degenerates of the
continent had first had the idea to make the befouled
stuff. It was for ponces in London, Pete said, it was
for criminals, it was for the kids he saw in prison. He
simply could not get his head, so he told us all, around
what 'all the fuss was about with bloody mayonnaise.'
The bar fell silent for a couple of minutes before a
conversation started up again. F1, no doubt. Or the
upcoming Six Nations game. I had thought of pointing
out to Pete that in fact the etymology of the word
'mayonnaise' itself may well involve the honouring of a
famous French victory over the British, that of then 3rd
Duke of Richelieu's in the Battle of Menorca in 1756.
But I thought better of it and stayed quiet once again.

* * * *

Over a period of a week or so, a few of the places on
the high street did indeed expand themselves out onto
the pavements as rumour had long promised. The deli,
the coffee shop and the Turkish restaurant all had

seating outside, and for a couple of weeks while the weather was fine, the village managed to maintain a certain Mediterranean air, with people sitting around luxuriating in the sun and, dare I say it, in the extra time they had on their hands. This, after all, was the definitive commuter location, with a good deal of the population of the place previously employed in London offices and now, presumably, finding themselves either furloughed or working from home. I did hear, through certain channels of gossip that pass inevitably through pub landlords like my father, that the Turkish restaurant had fallen foul of the rather pompous and self-important parish council types due to their enthusiastic use of banners and signs advertising their new, street-friendly offerings. A large plastic banner, for instance, had gone up on the front of the building advertising hot dogs and beef burgers. The councillor my father had spoken to had grumbled that it looked like something from the 'fucking funfair'. And we all knew how most of the villagers felt about the people who ran the funfair. For my part, I obviously enjoyed certain noses being put out of joint, and I was not averse to an ice cream from the restaurant's new machine. The councillor in question was, as I say, a rather unlikeable sort when he came in the pub. Over-officious about the pub quiz, for example. Liable to bring his beer back if the head wasn't quite right.

The building next door to the Turkish restaurant, though now closed for business, was a bridal shop called Le Sposi. Nothing of note about that, save for its zealous alarm, which had a peculiarly nocturnal habit of going off at random. But for most of my childhood and up until only a few years ago, this shop space, which made the corner of the high street and the London road that ran down to the Lantern, had been a bookshop. The owner of the shop, while he still lived here, cut something of a dash in the village, his hair long and curly, his glasses a nod to John Lennon. He ran, concurrently for a short time, another bookshop in Oxford where I had given a poetry reading once, back when I cared for such things, or more accurately I should say when such things cared for me. Once, when I must have been bemoaning some regular of the pub or other to him, the bookshop owner told me of a book that I should try and find in the local section of the library, the memoirs of a man called Spencer Thornton, who had once been vicar in the village, written by a William Robert Fremantle. Thornton had taken up his position after completing his degree at Cambridge in 1836, and at least according to Fremantle's book had promised, in what seemed to me to be an auspiciously dismal turn of phrase, to observe the anniversary of his appointment to the village as an 'anniversary of humiliation, and self-examination, and prayer'. At the time that Fremantle wrote his history, 1,200 of the 1,920 people named as residents of the place lived in the village proper, the rest littered around the surrounding countryside and dubbed 'The Foreign'. These were living in what the vicar's biographer believed to be a state of some neglect and poverty – living out hard, godless lives in huts in the hills – and the reverend appeared to have found the residents of the village, 'foreign' or otherwise, to have been a rather hard parish to break. Firstly, it seemed that they had been rather diligently profaning the sanctity of the Sabbath. The memoir mentioned one of Thornton's sermons lamenting the fact that work was routinely being done on Sundays – wages were being paid, farmhands had been seen in the fields, shops had been open, servants given a full list of tasks to be undertaken. More keenly felt than this transgression, however, was his 'aggressive movement against the habit of intemperance', which, it would seem, was reassuringly endemic to the place even as long ago as that. Thornton formed a local branch of the Church of England Total Abstinence Society and delivered numerous sermons on the subject. I found, upon reading those sermons that the vicar published, a curious blend of ideas of labour and work in his moral stand against the evils of alcohol. He asked what shall be said to shame those who 'do evil with both hands in earnest', 'who work all uncleanness with greed', 'practising the works of the flesh which are described Gal. v. 19, 20, 21.' He wrote of the 'profane oaths and filthy language of the idlers who flock together at the Market-house', 'rioting and drunkenness', 'domestic differences, misdemeanours and assaults', 'dishonest dealings, poaching and thieving', 'bad companions and idleness and mischief'. Thornton died young,

even by the standards of his day, and his memoir was
Fremantle's testament to what were undoubtedly
thought of as the good works of that short life, but
I read it as yet another artefact of the motifs and
patterns that weave themselves into the sites and
localities that we come to know. The patterning of
behaviour and experience, of sensation, of emotion.
The closeness of our own to the lives of the past which
these glimpses through language provided us. The
morality and manners were just the window frame
through which real lives could perhaps be seen. There
was a vitality to Fremantle's sentences the moment he
lit upon the riots and fairgrounds and public houses,
huts in the hills and slops and crime, and his words
became bloodless the moment he was back on more
stately ground. I remember a phrase the owner of the
bookshop wrote in a letter to me sometime after he'd
sold the shop and moved away. He was remembering
the regulars at the Lantern, with no real fondness,
having fallen out with one or two in his time. What a
shambolic lot they were, he wrote to me, made worse
by their respectability which, mostly, never collapsed
properly into destitute alcoholism.

* * * *

At the foot that led up to Aston Hill you could take
yourself through a half-hidden metal gate in the hedge
that ran up the incline to the top of the woods. On
the other side of the hedge, the ground gave way to a

series of irregular mounds, covered in short grass and wildflowers. Patches of gorse. Spears of purple and little pools of yellow. The rather peculiar undulations of the landscape were created when this area was a chalk quarry, and the land, since the work there ceased, had become a largely overlooked nature reserve called the Ragpits. Cars drove past and headed up to the top of the hill where there was a car park and a café and toilets. Dog walkers, and zip lines in the trees. All that was to be found down here, after all, were slow worms and voles, if you picked up the small squares of corrugated iron that had been left out to provide shade and shelter. A challenge to the kestrels in the daylight hours, and tawny owls at night. But the real attraction of this patch of land – the thing that was advertised on the little board as you walked through the gate – was its wild orchids. These plants, including very rare examples like the military orchid, were another characteristic feature of the hills in this area. I had always thought it a little odd that this strip of hills and chalk, written off everywhere as a slightly suburban non-entity, as a land of golf courses and safe Tory seats, of weekend car-washing and commuting, also offered such particular and overlooked biological riches. We had our handful of walkers in the pub at weekends, enjoying their sandwiches and their half pints of bitter shandy, but I wondered how many of the residents of the villages around here knew the nature of all that they lived with, day after day, week after week. This wasn't the Scottish Highlands, after all, or

the Lakes, or the Cornish Coast. We weren't sold the
idea that this was a locus of interest, of veneration.
And because we weren't told to, we didn't experience
the area in that way. But my notes told me otherwise.
They read pyramidal, greater butterfly, early purple,
bee and chalk fragrant – and there was more than
enough in those names before I even got to the birds
and butterflies and the fat, pale Roman snails that
proliferated here and which Monkey Wrench Mark
would sometimes take home for the pot.

* * * *

After a couple of weeks, the Turkish restaurant indeed
fell foul of the Parish Council, and was ordered to take
its furniture off the pavement and its banners and
signage off the walls. It was all above board, of course,
nothing to do with ideas of foreignness or those who do
or do not belong. All about the legalities of the place's
licence to sell alcohol. The last day that they had the
chairs outside, the local pop star pulled up in a green
Lamborghini and parked outside. It was about half ten
in the morning. He sat in one of the little metal seats
and ordered a bottle of beer. I watched from a bench
in the market square as he drank it back and ordered
another. He took the second with him and got back
into his car, revved the engine dismissively and roared
off into the hills, back to his hut.

* * * *

Inn-dependence Day. Super Saturday. The end
of the lockdown brought to you by the marketing
department of England. A week or so previously, the
government had announced they were to reopen the
pubs and proceeded to market the fact like a televised
sporting event – the ultimate cultural-capitalist
signifier of our degraded age. Viewed critically they
could have been said to have begun a project late
in the previous year, beginning with the very word
'government', to undermine, or to deconstruct the
very processes which lent the name, to the point
where it felt a stretch to use it, and now meant people
largely played the risks of the disease off against
their own individual financial opportunities, or social
needs, made their own decisions and calculations,
the guidance long since given up as bluff or bullshit,
the gestures of support for key workers or the NHS
turned squalid and platitudinous in an air, so recently
cleared of pollution, now thick with hypocrisy and
spleen. The backdrop to the biggest global public
health crisis in a generation was an utterly degraded
American political landscape, mounting tensions on
various Chinese borders, rumours of underage girls
manipulated into sex parties involving oligarchs,
magnates and minor royals, openly racist and violent
police forces, the super-rich profiteering from a
disease that had somehow, almost as if by design (and
the likes of Monkey Wrench Mark, with his Dark
Web fantasies of unseen controlling classes, no doubt
believed the fact), hit hardest among those already

most put upon. Each generation, so they say, feels
as if they are living through the end of history, but
I found myself wondering if things had ever felt this
overwhelmingly degenerate.

In the Lantern, the seating had been reorganised,
spaced out, more tables set up outside. Hand-sanitiser
on a small round table by the gents, more behind
the bar. Bottles of disinfectant to hand. The dray
had delivered its first beer since the closure all those
weeks ago, the cellar was organised, the whole place
was as clean as I could remember it being. The rooms
had taken on something of their old aspect, seemed
to anticipate the coming of people, of conversation,
of the obscure meaning communal spaces somehow
transmitted. Chairs were back behind tables, the
evidence of mine and my mother and father's domestic
life here moved back upstairs, back out of sight.

The morning itself was grey but dry. I woke early
and walked downstairs. Out of the back door, across
the road, up into the hills. There was something final
about my steps – something I could not name, could
not quite place, had shifted. When the pub first closed
its doors those months ago, I had often wondered
what it would feel like when we eventually reopened.
I imagined a profound sense of relief, of a certain
excitement, blended and perhaps even augmented by
the sadness attendant with the losses people would
have experienced. There would, I thought, inevitably

be some devastation close to home. But we would be back together in our places, remembering how we arranged ourselves in pews, or the plastic seats of sports stadia, around restaurant tables or at bars, in theatres or little clubs. So our losses and grief might be felt communally, as collective experience. As it happened the day felt strangely anti-climactic. The news surrounding the whole thing carried an undertone of disapproval. A terminally divided society could not, it turned out, experience loss or ecstasy collectively. Perhaps that was the job of time, or history – to smooth over the complications of an infinite number of highly individuated experiences and so turn discrete, complicated circumstance into public myth. And so we believed, on some level, that our wars, our depressions, our boom times, our pandemics were suffered or enjoyed by all. The philosophical mendacity that had soaked so deep into our national myth-making made deluded idiots of us all.

On the internet I saw people making the kind of easy, oppositional arguments that had so devalued public discussion over the previous few years. Go to the pubs when they reopened, some said, and you were contributing directly to the death toll, you were irresponsible at best, and at worst an openly callous, craven hypocrite, a racist, a murderer, a suicide, a member of a death cult. Millions of specific, different, individual experiences of the lockdown, and of its half-hearted, rather piecemeal easing off, millions of experiences of social and material loss, of isolation, of the impact on people's livelihoods and culture and human interactions being stripped away, and yet the debate had turned an infinitely complicated set of ideas into simplistic binaries of 'right' and 'wrong'. For my part, I could not begin to parse it. I had begun to experience all my feelings and my thoughts in those days through a fog of confusion, of half-formation, perhaps it was because of a half-heartedness of my own. I had lost any rigour I once had in my thinking, any passion I once had in my feeling. Perhaps the sharpening effect of conversation is what had denuded my thought, perhaps constant exposure to the news, to social media, the internet. Whatever it was, I felt a kind of fatigue. Or perhaps I was being overrun by the ghosts of this particular place – passivity, malaise, stagnation.

I walked the Ridgeway that morning with a sense of finality upon me. Finality to what, I could not quite say. With the pub reopening that afternoon, it felt as if this sliver of my life was coming to an end, this period of a solitude the likes of which I had not previously known, and yet had somehow always in some strange way anticipated. I walked through the grounds at Chequers, past the box wood and Happy Valley and out to Whiteleaf Cross, a large chalk hill carving in the scarp overlooking a neighbouring village. It was an oddly proportioned, triangular-based image of a cross, perhaps in imitation of a church building that

the village once lacked, a gesture towards the spired
skyline that once marked most of the settlements in
the area. Nobody really knew when or how the cross
was made but there were many stories. My favourite
postulation, though, and a common one in the pub, was
that originally the carving was a pagan fertility symbol
that was later 'Christianised' – an enormous cock-
and-balls in the hillside that had offended Victorian
sensibilities and so had to be altered. Of course
there was no evidence to back the story up, but it
played easily to the kind of simplified ideas of certain
historical periods that people seem so keen to believe
in. A sexualised paganism and a prim Victoriana. The
cross was featured in a number of paintings by Paul
Nash, despite not having acquired the same prestige
as the white horse at Uffington, which could be seen a
number of miles further along the Ridgeway. I sat at
the top of the cliff and drank from my flask of coffee.
Kites and crows had followed me along the path all
morning. Jackdaws half-cackled in groups of half a
dozen. Young birds, perhaps. The year had mostly
spent its birdsong now, though a goldfinch piped up
from the gorse and flew away as I walked past. That
morning the path through the woods was quiet of
human life too, the hills emptied, perhaps as people
began once more to live out a version of their old
lives. Weekend processions along the high streets and
supermarkets and shopping centres. The sports clubs
had begun to gear up, the kids needing to be taken to
matches and training. Dinner parties, BBQs, camping

holidays. The old diversions of work and social and family life would begin to resurface in the patterns of people's time. Sunday would take back its old and rightful melancholy. Friday afternoon its old and delicious enchantment.

Walking back along the path, down in the gulch at the base of Whiteleaf Hill, I came to a pub that had, much like The Paper Lantern, appeared in its little clearing among the beech trees these last weeks as a kind of spectre on my walks. Each time I passed it I thought of the opening lines of Edward Thomas's poem 'Up in the Wind' – more white horses, more chalk. A public house that 'may be public for birds, / Squirrels and such-like, ghosts of charcoal-burners / And highwaymen.' How could he know it, all those years ago and miles away? Of course he had walked this way himself, once, maybe more, and written his own book about travelling these paths. The village got a passing mention as a 'long little town', and in the edition we kept in the pub there was a scratchy illustration of the high street. Here for most of the previous weeks, this pub's outdoor furniture had been piled up in the garden as if awaiting the bonfire or the fire sale. The windows dark and dusty. Today, though, there was a kind of reanimation. The furniture was set out once more, the door open, the yellowed light of the tavern windows offered its particular welcome, even in the full daylight of the hour I walked past. I contemplated stopping for a drink. This pub, of course, had its own stories, its own lore. On the internet it proclaimed itself 'probably the most famous pub in England', and that might well be true, though these things don't always mean what they might. Most people remembered the pub, for instance, as the place where, while he was prime minister and staying at Chequers, David Cameron and his wife left their daughter behind after having lunch. I remembered the talk of it at the time, insipidly good-natured, round here where David Cameron could largely have done no wrong in the eyes of most. Who hadn't left something behind in the pub after a few too many over lunch? Almost funny to think that in many ways wrong is *all* Cameron had now been seen to do. Divisions across the country opened up by his disastrous decision to call a referendum on Europe, HS2 bulldozing through ancient woodland and the Tory heart of middle England, but most of all, there was a sense that he was the blueprint for a specific sort of privately wealthy politician-as-mediocrity, an urtext version of the talentless figures that had, in those times, emptied their office of so much of its previous and, one might be tempted to believe, actually quite necessary, esteem in the perception of the populace. No matter their broad political or party-political allegiances, it was hard to find anyone, even here in the right-wing badlands, who wouldn't simply sigh into their pint and tell you across the bar that they've 'had it with the lot of them' or some such phrase. They were simply spivs who had long sold the country a parochial caricature of itself, under the guise of what Cameron's own tutor at Oxford had once described as his 'sensible Conservative views', and they had then looked on as that sensibility was co-opted and moulded into a small-minded, reactionary, nationalistic nervous breakdown. These were the people who *knew* that for money and so, for those that possess money in the requisite quantity, borders meant precisely nothing. Continents, nations, regions, zones, blocs — simply more meaningless symbols, more categorical sleight-of-hand, the illusion of an order, of 'reason', of histories that could be put to work. I thought of how, after a state visit from the Chinese president in 2015, and with Cameron and Xi Jinping photographed with fish and chips and pints of brown beer, this little pub out here in a bland suburban wood, became an improbable tourist destination for Chinese visitors. In fact, a short while later, or so the rumours were, a Chinese property and investment company had bought the pub, and took the landlord at the time on as a kind of consultant, helping them to open a chain of English-style pubs across China. I would think of that when I walked past, or occasionally stopped for a beer. I thought of how at the very same time, there might have been any number of versions of this very pub sign above a door in Beijing, someone ordering a pint however many thousands of miles away, and taking that first gratifying drink. Perhaps we could be forgiven for not seeing the signs back then, subtle as they were, that we were heading for our current degradation. The pig's heads, the forgotten children, the open, celebratory nepotisms, the clubbishness of it all. These are my own categorisations of course, littered among these rather mean-spirited words, my own reductive and ultimately inarticulate grumblings.

I carried on past the pub, no stopping for a beer this time, and took myself back to the village. The road at the bottom of the ridge was busy once again, the golf course at the foot of Coombe Hill dotted with players like any Saturday from the time before the virus. Small groups of expensive bicycles rode past bearing their riders in bright Lycra. A dog or two by the monument, a group of teenagers with a picnic blanket and a few cans. I walked with a strange, and rather dislocated awareness of these scenes as I saw them, as if I were rebuilding images of the place backward out of memory. There was nothing of menace here, nothing of anger, of disease, of death, of heartbreak. And yet at the same time nothing of joy, of relief, of wonder, of abandon. The figures seemed still, the faces blank. The ground passed without impediment under me, my feet felt as though they were hardly touching the earth. Beech trees at my side. Willowherb, gorse, the first brambles. Peacock and red admiral butterflies fought over the flowers. At the foot of the hill I reached the tarmac of the road. I passed the Railway Hotel, the little row of cottages on my right. I turned into South Street and saw the A-frame standing outside the front of the pub which said, simply, 'Welcome

Back'. I walked up the road and through the front
doors. I saw the Mexican ornaments above the bar,
the old Metro-land travel posters on the wall, the
map of the Thames valley, the black and white
photographs of country music stars from the sixties.
I felt, quite suddenly and quite acutely, the tang
of this place in particular. The material fact of it.
I thought once more about the meaninglessness of
words in the face of things, how they continue to
slip out of the grasp of the mind. A pint of Landlord,
please, landlord, I heard myself say to the man behind
the bar, who was also my father.